IN SEARCH
+ OF THE +
KNIGHTS
TEMPLAR

Simon Brighton was born in London but brought up in Lincolnshire, in the shadow of the Temple Bruer, one of the most important Templar sites in the country. He became fascinated by the Knights at an early age and has pursued that fascination ever since. Simon has meticulously researched and documented each of the key British sites and his photographs were included in the illustrated edition of *The Da Vinci Code*.

IN SEARCH
+OF THE+
KNIGHTS TEMPLAR

A GUIDE
TO THE SITES
IN BRITAIN

SIMON
BRIGHTON

Contents

FOREWORD

As I was growing up in Lincolnshire, I would often go past an ancient solitary tower standing within a farm in Temple Bruer, about a mile to the north of my family's house just outside the village of Brauncewell. I learned that it was built by people called 'the Templars', but initially knew nothing more. I had heard them mentioned in general conversation and remember placing them with the other big historical landowning families. Like most young boys, I was intrigued by castles and ruins — and the tower doubly so, because even at a young age I was aware that it was a mysterious place. I don't remember any specific ghost stories or scary anecdotes but I do recall the eerie fascination the old ruin held for me.

By the time I was fourteen, in 1973, I wanted to know more about this unique ruin, and visited the library in nearby Sleaford. The librarian couldn't have been more helpful, digging out some dusty volumes — none of them less than a century old—and leaving me to read.

I learnt of the travels of William Stukeley, who in the seventeenth century described the Roman road of Ermine Street running just to the west of Brauncewell. This, he said, was the main road from London to York, and at the crossroads near the tower he saw an ancient standing stone on which the Templars had carved their distinctive cross. And I read nineteenth-century accounts of the history of Lincolnshire, with references to the Templars' presence — how they established themselves in the county, making the lands here some of their most productive, but had then been extinguished by the Pope and the French king. Their properties outlasted them and were pressed into the service of others. Henry VIII had stayed at the Temple Bruer tower, though it was in a ruinous state even then, and his staff had to erect huge marquees to keep him comfortable.

Finally, I read of the survey of the tower undertaken in 1841 by a Reverend Oliver. In the 'preceptory of the knights Templar' he found walled-up bodies and evidence of dark practices in secret chambers, along with tunnels built by the Templars leading under the fields to nearby villages — in short, just the sort of gothic information I was looking for!

Thirty years ago, there was little general information on the Templars to redress what I had read, so I was allowed to reflect on the lurid details, and cheerfully relate them to anyone who would listen. Our house, secluded and ancient itself, was on a hill, and without electricity. So visiting friends could be scared half to death by my embellished stories of the sinister Templars, before they were given oil lamps and directed to their bedrooms.

But within this youthful research I had also learnt historical facts: why so many of the local

Below The remains of the Lincolnshire preceptory of Temple Bruer standing within Temple Farm.

villages had French names; how the Templars farmed the land, and had their headquarters in London; about the Crusades and an order of knights who crossed the line and said they would be willing to die rather than abandon God's work. These knights had lived close to my house, owned property in my village and trained their cavalry in the field next door. To me these knights seemed far more 'real' than the history I was learning at school.

And I began to comprehend that the lone tower just up the road was really an outpost of Jerusalem, built to sustain a conflict hundreds of miles away.

Later, in 1982, a book called *The Holy Blood and the Holy Grail* would augment my knowledge with more sensational details of the knights, and their alleged secret ambitions to secure one of the holiest relics of Christendom.

During the 1980s I started to visit prehistoric sites with my friend Terry, taking a kind of trainspotterish approach, ticking off stone circles and burial chambers as we travelled the length and breadth of the country. But soon I began to supplement the stone circles with Templar sites and, with a growing interest in photography, started to record my travels. So I had a ready supply of photographs when the Templar expert and web pioneer Tim Staniland put out a request for pictures for his 'Templars in Britain' site. Through this site many people started getting in contact with me and asking if I knew about sites they had discovered.

Above A romantic vision of a Templar in full regalia.

The advent of digital photography allowed images to be captured in almost impossible conditions, such as near dark crypts. I could then study these photos back at home, often discovering features I hadn't noticed, which I could investigate further on a repeat visit to the site.

In 2000 George Tull's ground-breaking book *The Traces of the Templars*, a guide to the sites in England, was published; a couple of years later, along came Evelyn Lord's *The Knights Templar in Britain*, a valuable source of information not available elsewhere at that time. With these two books permanently in the glove compartment of my car, I spent as much time visiting the sites as I could, and soon had enough photos and local information to make the idea of writing a book a real possibility.

✠ THIS BOOK is essentially observational, the images and text generated by the individual sites. As each location is unique, I could emphasise a particular theme related within the text, so for example Templecombe with its painting of the 'Head' is related to the Templars' alleged worship of heads, while Temple Bruer is concerned with their agricultural achievements, and a

Templar hostel such as Strood provides the opportunity to consider the 'travel agency' services the Order provided.

I am not a historian and have no particular 'angle' on the Templars, other than finding them endlessly fascinating. I do not wish to denigrate the work of others, whether orthodox, academic or speculative. Nor do I take sides in any controversy. If the Templars were indeed after the Ark of the Covenant, that pursuit should not detract from their achievements within medieval society and their place in military history. And conversely, that they were wealthy and became the elite of their day in various secular matters does not mean they were similarly 'orthodox' in spiritual practice.

A final note: recently, along with my friend Terry and his dog, I walked northwards along Ermine Street, to visit the tower at Temple Bruer using the old Templar route. As we were walking, the dog — young and boisterous — seemed not to have a care in the world, running and jumping with abandon. But, once we got near the tower, it was a different story. He refused to enter the ruin, and when either of us went in he yelped for us to come out. And all at once I remembered the stories of walled-up bodies, satanic practices and secret tunnels that the Reverend Oliver had described and that had so engrossed my young self...

SIMON BRIGHTON,
London, Spring 2006

INTRODUCTION

THE KNIGHTS TEMPLAR DAZZLED THE MEDIEVAL WORLD in which they flourished, and left a legacy that has lingered down the centuries, captivating generations with their power, their glamour, and their final mystery. ✚ They truly were a giant of their time: the first uniformed standing army since the days of the Roman Empire and, off the battlefield, the first truly multinational organisation. Great landowners, industrialists and traders, the knights also introduced banking, the linchpin of the modern world, to Europe. In an astonishingly swift rise from the early twelfth century, they amassed huge wealth and exerted corresponding power, their leaders walking with kings and princes and enjoying the favour of popes. ✚ In less than two hundred years, they were gone. ✚ And ever since, the Knights Templar have existed more in fiction than in fact, their history woven into myth and fantasy, their reputation twisted this way and that to suit prejudice and superstition — or just to make a good story. Their fellow fighting monks, the Knights Hospitaller, followed a less controversial path, the Order existing today in humanitarian bodies such as the Red Cross and St John Ambulance — and are universally admired. Why should the Hospitallers' medieval contemporaries have had such a dramatically different fate? ✚ The Templars' end was as sudden as their rise: the once mighty Order denounced and suppressed, its property seized and reassigned, its members scattered, reduced to seeking refuge abroad or confined in squalid dungeons, subjected to inhuman torture before enduring the flames of execution. In effect, the Knights Templar were obliterated and, as ever, the victors wrote the history. Around the official version of their fate, rumour and speculation about this extraordinary body of men have abounded to this day. ✛

THE TEMPLARS IN HISTORY

Just as the knights' end is shrouded in mystery, so is their beginning. They kept little or no records themselves — these fighting men were unlike their cloistered brethren and had a reputation for scorning the written word. The first accounts did not appear until decades after the Order had come into being, and these early chronicles were by no means impartial. The ostensible reason seems eminently plausible, though: the Templars were founded to provide protection for the city and for Christian pilgrims in the Holy Land after Jerusalem was conquered by Christians in 1099.

The Holy Land (modern Israel and Lebanon) had long been a volatile battleground between Christians and Muslims. The new faith of Islam had spread rapidly east and west from the Arabian peninsula until, in 637, its warriors took control of Jerusalem itself. Before then, it had been held mainly by Byzantine Christians, whose empire had grown out of the failing Roman Empire when it was split into east and west in AD 395. The eastern empire's capital, Byzantium, was renamed Constantinople by the emperor Constantine the Great, who had made Christianity the official religion of the Roman Empire in 312. It was during his reign that certain holy sites were identified — according to legend by his mother, St Helena — many of them in Jerusalem.

These were the sites that were to make up the pilgrimage trail, with western Christians being eager to follow in the footsteps of Christ. In fact it became a regular activity, an organised enterprise throughout Christendom. Hostelries were set up along the way, tolls were charged, and guides were available. This continued even after the Muslims' conquest of 637. Although they did not stop fighting their enemies, in the main they did allow Christians to live and worship freely.

This freedom ended in 1071 when nomadic Seljuk Turks, converts to Sunni Islam, decisively defeated the Byzantines in battle, captured Jerusalem and expelled their rival Muslims. The Seljuks did not have the tolerance of their predecessors, and began to harry Christians. Pilgrims especially had always been a soft target, travelling through a harsh land beset with bandits. Now the Seljuks made life even more difficult for them, not least in charging extortionate fees to access holy sites.

Above The legendary foundation of Christianity as a state religion: Constantine defeats Maximus in AD 312 at the Battle of Malvern Bridge and puts his victory down to a newfound faith in Christ.

Right Pilgrim marks – the cross potent, a symbol of Jerusalem. These were carved at Bellapais Abbey, Cyprus.

Previous page Effigies of Templar Knights found in Temple Church, London. The one in the foreground is that of Gilbert Marshal, fourth Earl of Pembroke; the other is unknown.

IN SEARCH OF THE KNIGHTS TEMPLAR

In 1095, the Byzantine emperor Alexis asked the Roman Pope, Urban II, for help. In November that year, in a field just outside the walls of the French city of Clermont-Ferrand, Urban answered the call with a sermon emphasising the dangers the pilgrims were experiencing and the desecration of the sacred sites in the Holy Land by the 'Mohammedans'. He called upon the congregation to 'take the cross' and journey to the East, with force of arms, to assist fellow Christians. And so began that series of expeditions at once idealistic and corrupt, devout and profane: the Crusades.

Urban's call met with an enthusiastic response from all parts of society, from the highest to the lowest. The lowest, however, had little hope of matching their zeal with effective action. They formed the majority of the first wave of 'crusaders': essentially a rabble, most of whom were massacred or died of disease along the way. The second wave in 1096 contained more of the higher classes of society; it was far better organised, with armed knights providing military muscle. This was the crusading force that fought its way through Asia Minor and finally captured Jerusalem in 1099,

Above left The People's Crusade of 1096. An undisciplined band of 25,000 peasants set off for the Holy Land. This manuscript shows them being attacked by Hungarians en route. Those who survived to cross the Mediterranean were massacred by the Turks. This bloody Crusade led to the formation of the Knights Templar, whose role would be to provide protection.
Above Godfrey de Bouillon enters Jerusalem in the First Crusade, as depicted in the 1877 book *Bibliothèque des Croisades* by J. F. Michaud.

indiscriminately massacring the inhabitants.

In the aftermath, the Kingdom of Jerusalem was set up, but its fragility was immediately apparent. Many of the crusaders returned home, and those who remained were hard pressed by hostile forces. It was increasingly clear that what was needed was an organised group of knights, who would be able to fight in a controlled way and respond to the varied needs of the occupiers.

Enter the Templars — but exactly how is unclear. The most detailed account of the Templars' foundation, though not corroborated elsewhere, comes from William, Archbishop of Tyre, in his *History of Deeds Done Beyond the Sea*, written some fifty years after the event. William describes how, in 1118, nine knights approached King Baldwin II of Jerusalem with a suggestion.

They would take the monastic vows of 'poverty, chastity and obedience' and found an order that concerned itself with protecting pilgrims arriving from the West and travelling along the routes from the coast. This would be no easy task: pilgrims had been attacked and killed in large numbers.

The names of the founding knights are uncertain, though the leader appears fairly consistently to be one Hugh de Payens. William of Tyre explains that the knights took their name from their quarters that Baldwin, agreeing to their request, had allocated them next to the Temple Mount in Jerusalem. As a result, they became known as the 'Poor Knights of Christ of the Temple of Solomon'. One illustration of their poverty was their early seal, depicting two brothers on a single horse (though of course this may also have indicated fellowship).

According to William, there were only these nine knights for the next nine years—years that have been the subject of much debate, arising chiefly from the location of their headquarters, the Temple Mount being a place of great significance to Jews, Christians and Muslims alike. The Mount is a part natural and part man-made platform, formed from an outcrop containing original chambers and excavated tunnels. In the time of the Templars these were said to house many holy relics—the greatest being the Ark of the Covenant.

Such stories would have been common knowledge to the Templars as well as other crusaders. Indeed, the Crusades were looked on by many of the Christians as an opportunity to liberate—or loot, depending on one's viewpoint—any holy relics found along the way.

Were the Templars, as has been suggested, the most organised band of looters of all the crusaders? Did they know through ancient wisdom exactly what they were looking for?

The truth of what is or was hidden within the Temple Mount will probably never be known, but what is certain is that the Templars were investigating

Above The early Templar seal inscribed SIGILLUM MILITUM XPISTI meaning 'sign of the army of Christ'. **Opposite left** Examples of the Templars' black and white banner, called the beauséant. **Opposite** Three romantic eighteenth-century depictions of Templars at work and prayer.

IN SEARCH OF THE KNIGHTS TEMPLAR

the underground chambers within the Mount. In 1894, a British lieutenant, Charles Wilson of the Royal Engineers, was working for the Ordnance Survey deep within the Mount, and discovered several Templar artefacts—a cross, a spur and a spear.

Whatever the Templars were doing there—and nobody knows for sure—they were ever after associated with mystical relics, mysterious powers, buried treasure ... perfect catalysts for endless speculation.

More prosaically, the decisive turn in their earthly fortunes came in 1127, when Hugh and some of his comrades went to France to appear at the Council of Troyes. Here, the fledgling Order—this novel hybrid of the monastic and the martial—gained the recognition of the pope, influenced, crucially, by the support of Bernard of Clairvaux. Bernard (later St Bernard), had reinvigorated the Cistercian Order, founding the monastery in Clairvaux, in the Champagne region of France, and was an extremely important figure.

Here, the Order was given its Rule, the precepts by which any monastic community was bound to live. Initially, it was based on the Benedictine model and prescribed every element of the members' lives: when to eat, when to pray, when to sleep, and so on—as well as the usual bans on impure conduct and contact with women. While this kind of discipline was

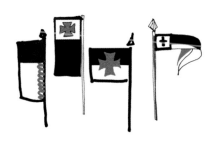

essential to define and bind any monastic order, it was especially vital for the Templars, whose community would transcend national boundaries. Furthermore, such military orders were governed by councils, who would in theory be able to make decisions based on rational strategy rather than the self-

interested or whimsical directions that nobles usually pursued.

One decision at the Council of Troyes was to have a profound effect on the Templars' fortunes—literally. The pope's favour made them answerable only to him, freeing them from local diocese control and taxes. This privilege was to excite much jealousy and resentment.

Another result of the Council was immediately visible: the knights' dress. For the previous nine years, they had not worn any distinguishing clothes. Now they were to wear a habit modelled on the Cistercian pattern of white mantle and white cloak—white of course being the symbol of purity. Ironically, this purity was not translated to personal hygiene. In fact Bernard of Clairvaux promoted them as the antithesis to the worldly knights who prided themselves on their appearance, being clean-shaven with flowing locks. The Templars cropped their hair and grew long raggedy beards, and thought washing an indulgence.

Only the knights were granted the white mantle. Those brothers lower in the hierarchy, sergeants and squires, wore darker colours. What became

their well-known red cross, called pattée, was added some twenty years later, positioned over the heart as a symbolic shield.

Whatever his habit, a fighter needed his sword. At the time of the Crusades, such arms — before the age of machined tools — were immensely valuable. (In fact any metal tool, whether weapon or farm implement, commanded a very high price. Twelfth-century audits equated the worth of the machinery and tools of a manor — such as ploughs and shears — with the worth of the manor and land themselves.) So a sword was by no means a weapon available to all. The ritual of carving the silhouette of the sword around the owner's grave slab testifies to the regard in which this weapon was held.

The crusaders' swords were different from those used by Celts and other earlier tribes, which were made of laminated metals and in fact resembled Saracen weapons. Here, strands of different kinds of iron would be wound and plaited, heated and beaten until a remarkably fine blade was created, with a razor-sharp edge. But such finesse was no good to a knight facing an opponent wearing armour — he needed more of a bludgeon to make an impact. Chain mail was the most successful defensive invention of the age. Made by twisting yards of iron wire around a metal tube, the twist would then be cut and the resulting rings interlinked. It was very effective in deflecting thrusts from sharp blades.

To combat chain mail, weapons became heavier. Battleaxes began to be used, and weighty swords were designed to hit with such an impact that even if the chain mail held, wounds would be inflicted — to the extent of incapacitating the victim.

During the lifetime of the Templars, armour became increasingly more elaborate and relied less on chain mail and more on helmets and body

Above A knight's sword, clearly outlined on the grave of its owner.
Right Detail of chain mail, also on a Templar tomb.

IN SEARCH OF THE KNIGHTS TEMPLAR

armour such as breast plates and arm guards. The plating was supposed to offer protection against the impact of heavy swords.

With all the plating and protection, a reasonable strategy was forcing an opponent to the ground, then using a small sharp dagger to thrust through the only vulnerable unguarded area: the eyepiece of the helmet. Eventually, the armour became so heavy that it was not uncommon for soldiers to suffocate in the heat of battle. (And even away from the battlefield, in tournaments, knights were sometimes asphyxiated.)

Saracens were more lightly armoured, just the coat of mail called a hauberk and a helmet. Their tactics would rely on speed and manoeuvrability. Using lighter, smaller horses, they were skilled at firing arrows while riding at speed, and trying to find the chinks in their opponents' armour with their fine blades.

There is a tale, often repeated and doubtless only a tale, that makes clear the difference between crusader and Saracen fighting style. This tells of Richard I of England—the 'Lionheart'—and Saladin, but could equally apply to any Frankish knight and Saracen warrior. They had met and enjoyed a meal and, as they sat at the table, the conversation turned to the weapons both employed.

Saladin explained how his sword was made through the superlative skill of the swordsmith, and he demonstrated its effectiveness. On his instruction a silk veil was thrown into the air, whereupon, without disturbing the descent of the silk, Saladin fizzed his blade through the air. When the silk came to rest it was observed to be in several pieces.

Above A fourteenth-century illustration of King Richard I of England – the 'Lionheart' – tilting at Saladin, the Sultan of Egypt and Syria.

In response, Richard arose, sword in hand, and with one blow smashed the table in two...

✝ DIRECTLY AFTER the Council of Troyes, Hugh de Payens travelled to Normandy, England and Scotland to cultivate support for the knights. This is mentioned in *The Anglo-Saxon Chronicle*:

> This same year came from Jerusalem Hugh of the Temple to the king in Normandy; and the king received him with much honour, and gave him rich presents in gold and in silver. And afterwards he sent him into England; and there he was received by all good men, who all gave him presents, and in Scotland also: and by him they sent to Jerusalem much wealth withal in gold and in silver.

'To Jerusalem' was the key: the whole point of the Templars' existence was to support the crusader states. When stationed abroad and not actually

Above A detail of a boat on a tomb contemporaneous with the Templars. Note the huge rudder on the right.

fighting the enemy, their every effort was to channel money back to the Holy Land, keeping only a bare subsistence for themselves. Within fifty years, they would build power bases throughout Europe, using their growing wealth to buy land and property, develop agriculture and industry, and build up a fleet of ships in which they could trade throughout the known world.

Meanwhile, their status as an elite fighting force was growing, involving them in campaigns beyond the Holy Land — most notably against the Moors in the Iberian peninsula. They were not the only military–religious order in action, but they were the first. The Knights Hospitaller had been formed before them but, as their name suggests, they worked first in a medical or pastoral capacity before becoming part of the military. Throughout Christendom the Hospitallers and Templars were able to coexist fairly amicably. Occasionally, though, they would find themselves embroiled in the internal quarrels of the Latin kingdoms—kings and nobles being particularly keen to benefit from them falling out with one another.

A third order, the Teutonic Knights, was formed much later, in 1190, and fought campaigns mostly in the Baltic region, 'converting' pagan Slavic tribes to Christianity.

The military orders soon proved themselves on the battlefield. Their skills were unsurpassed for their age and, mounted—in contrast to the Saracens— on heavy horses, they were a formidable force, sweeping away their opponents. Templars would have favoured the stocky chargers of the time. Most knights' horses were not like the thoroughbreds seen at the races today; they would need to have the crucial qualities of stamina, temperament, speed and agility. An example of the crusaders' mount was the Ardennes heavy horse, as Tim Severin's research for his book *Crusader* revealed. It was the equivalent of a heavy tank, weighing as much as a ton and able to run at 20 mph, described as 'sober and robust ... renowned for its toughness, its ability to withstand all kinds of climate, its eagerness to work and its frugal feeding'. These warhorses were so effective that later they became subject to a form of early arms control through royal edict—the purpose being to limit access to the breed, in the knowledge that a cavalry charge on these horses was virtually unstoppable.

The Templars were after all predominantly a cavalry troop, as knights of the time were. From stations such as Penhill in Yorkshire and stud farms in

IN SEARCH OF THE KNIGHTS TEMPLAR

Ireland, they would have had to train, breed and ship their horses to the East.

Apart from their formidable power on horseback, these trained, organised knights were a new phenomenon in that they fought in formation and, crucially, were willing to die in the process. A secular knight was unlikely to be killed in battle and expected to be protected by his enemy for the ransom. He might be imprisoned for a while, but to die on the field of battle would not profit anyone. A Templar might be taken captive, but could expect no ransom.

Though the Templars relied on the cavalry charge where possible, it was obviously a high-risk strategy and, if it went wrong, large numbers of mounted knights, a most valuable resource, would be lost. Contrary to common perception, few armies of the time wished to engage in battle—the risks were too great. Even the victor would usually have sustained losses that would be hard to replace. A much more conservative strategy would be the siege, a gradual process of attrition that could on occasion take years, but it did allow the adversaries time to assess their position and, if appropriate, make terms. The history of the Crusades consists of a series of sieges undertaken by both sides.

Below The Templars' Castle Almoural in Portugal. Built on an island, although occasionally besieged, it was never taken by force. Now owned by the military, it is open to the public.

The Templars would not always resort to either siege or battle. Committed to the maintenance of the Kingdom of Jerusalem by any means, they also pursued the diplomatic route. The Order gained a reputation for pragmatism and caution, deploying strategy and negotiation rather than force, making alliances with local Muslim leaders and employing local people. Many of the brothers learned Arabic, and gained an appreciation of sophisticated Islamic culture, which in many respects—not least scholarship and medicine—was more advanced than its western counterpart.

The Arabic libraries had the translations of the Greek philosophers that the West had lost; taken back to Europe, they would provide the impetus for the Renaissance. As for medicine, one Muslim warrior and courtier, Usmah ibn Munqidh, related a telling anecdote in his autobiography, *A Muslim on the Franks*, dated around 1175. With a highly developed understanding of the human body, he was beneficially treating a knight and a woman for their ills until he was forcefully replaced by a 'Frankish physician' whose brutal and ignorant methods promptly killed the patients. 'Thereupon I asked them whether my services were needed any longer, and when they replied in the negative I returned home, having learned of their medicine what I knew not before.'

With their pragmatic openness to new ideas, the knights also took from Islam the concept of banking—something that would consolidate their power in the medieval world. Taking currency from one place to another was fraught with the usual dangers of theft and, when travelling abroad, shipwreck. If a traveller could safely deposit a sum of money at one end of his journey and, presenting a coded note at the other end, receive the same amount (less commission), then a whole new world of commerce could open up. There was also some life assurance in this process: if the traveller died before he returned home, the Templars would make some provision for his family out of the funds he had deposited.

Once the Templars had established their network of properties, ports and ships throughout Europe and the Holy Land, they were in a position to facilitate all manner of services—not just as bankers, but travel agents,

Right A continuing testament to the Templars' wealth, the magnificent Temple Church in London.

hoteliers, shippers, and traders in import–export. It would be possible, say, for a potential crusader in Lincolnshire to deposit some funds at the Templars' Temple Bruer, travel across Europe staying at Templar properties and using Templar ships, until he arrived in Jerusalem and withdrew his money, thankful to the Templars for the discounts they offered and happy to allow them their percentage.

The Templars were becoming a genuine multinational organisation, with the purpose of maintaining the crusader states. They were also, incidentally, fuelling rumours of their great wealth. As ever, where actual knowledge of their activities was patchy, envy and resentment would readily fill the gaps — while their use of coded promissory notes, essential for security, added to their reputation for secrecy.

Their conduct in the Holy Land would also be fertile ground for those wishing to spread rumours. While their strategy was contributing to a relatively settled period in the history of the Kingdom of Jerusalem, their role of negotiators made enemies of the more reactionary elements in the crusading armies. The Templars were 'going native'—arousing the suspicion of heresy that would eventually be instrumental in their downfall.

Meanwhile, newer crusaders were arriving from the West, with no interest in blending into the multicultural population of the Holy Land—they were after power and land. So, just as the kingdom looked as though there was a possibility of a sustained peace, ambitious, warlike knights were arriving to stir things up again, fighting among themselves, and displaying poor judgement leading to disastrous strategic decisions.

Above *La Perte de la Sainte Croix* (The Loss of the Holy Cross). This French manuscript shows the capture of Jerusalem by Saladin in 1187.

Meanwhile, their enemy was growing in strength. Under the sultan Saladin, who united previously warring factions, Muslim forces decisively defeated a Christian army at the Horns of Hattin in 1187. Surviving Christians were allowed to go — with the exception of hundreds of military knights. Saladin had as his guests at this time a party of Sufis, travelling teachers known for their wisdom. To them Saladin allocated the task of executing the knights (perhaps he thought they needed a touch of reality). So he and his men were entertained by the sight of the untrained, bookish Sufis inexpertly wielding swords at the unfortunate knights.

Saladin was known for his compassion and chivalry so, whatever his motive in using the Sufis, his treatment of the knights showed that he viewed them as his main threat. Here he tore out the heart of the military orders.

After this victory, Saladin and his forces went on to take Jerusalem in October of that year. It was the beginning of the end for Christians in the Holy Land.

The crusader kingdoms limped on — there was even a truce in 1192 between Saladin and Richard I of England. But throughout the next century, as new waves of crusaders challenged Saladin's successors, the Christians slowly but inexorably lost ground. On 18 May 1291, the last crusader port, Acre, was lost.

The crusaders established a kingdom-in-waiting on Cyprus, with the king of the island being given the title 'king of Jerusalem', but it gradually became clear that Jerusalem would not be regained, and the desire to engage in yet more crusades waned.

The Templars had bought Cyprus from Richard I in 1191, but felt able to devote only a small number of inexperienced men to it. Soon there was an insurrection, and the knights saw the island as a burden rather than an opportunity. They decided to sell it back to Richard, who by chance was indebted to one Guy de Lusignan. The English king repaid him by facilitating his purchase of Cyprus, bankrolled by the Italian traders. Guy would found a dynasty that ruled the island for over three hundred years, further accentuating the chance missed by the Templars, who could have established a Templar state, much as the Hospitallers managed to do on the smaller island of Rhodes. As John J. Robinson wrote, 'the great tragedy of the Templars

Above Shields of the Lusignan family, the medieval rulers of Cyprus. The dynasty was founded by Guy de Lusignan, who was seen as an exiled king in waiting after the fall of Jerusalem. Yet Jerusalem was never to be retaken. **Right** Two chapels side-by-side in Famagusta. The left-hand one is said to be Templar, the right Hospitaller.

IN SEARCH OF THE KNIGHTS TEMPLAR

was the failure to hold on to Cyprus' — an island rich in resources and strategically placed to access the ports of Egypt, Palestine and Byzantium.

The only order to maintain a presence in the East was the Knights Hospitaller, who remained on Rhodes until 1522 when Turks seized the island. They then moved on to Malta, where they flourished as traders — dealing among other profitable commodities in slaves, the foundation of many cities —until they were evicted by Napoleon. By now, the Reformation in England and a move to the Protestant faith elsewhere diminished the influence of the Hospitallers, who eventually became the Knights of St John, caring for the sick and injured, and founded St John Ambulance in the UK.

The other military order founded at the time of the Crusades, the Teutonic Knights, has also survived into modern times in various incarnations, and is now a religious charitable institution based in Vienna.

While the Hospitallers and the Teutonic Knights were destined for long centuries of service, the Templars' light was to be suddenly extinguished.

✝ THE TEMPLARS' EXISTENCE was intrinsically bound up with defence of the Holy Land. When that was lost, they were seen, if not as actually responsible, at least as failures, increasingly redundant, especially when in 1305 they declined the opportunity to merge with the Knights Hospitaller. The Templars, increasingly perceived as anachronistic, were leaving themselves open to attack. The fourteenth century was starting on its devastating path of widespread wars, and plagues presaging the Black Death itself. Populations had enough to manage without being taxed for far-flung crusades—and in any case, the monastic movement generally was losing public support, the orders viewed as avaricious and selfish, typified by the caricature of the fat lazy monk. Several English monasteries had to build defences to keep out unhappy locals.

Meanwhile, the avaricious and impulsive French king saw his chance to attack the isolated Order. Philip IV (called 'the Fair') had reigned since 1285, and had long nursed resentment of the Templars' power and reputed wealth. A few years earlier he had apparently been rejected when he applied to become a member of the Order, and had borrowed heavily from them.

He could achieve the two aims of removing them as a political threat and gaining their property, if he could find an excuse to attack them. He had a useful ally in the Pope, Clement V, who had been elected in 1305. The Vatican being as riven with violence and factions as any secular state, Rome had grown too hot for the pontiff, who accepted Philip's offer of a breakaway refuge in Avignon. So Clement was effectively under the control of Philip, and appeared to support him in his campaign to suppress the Templars.

Philip laid his plans well—and secretly. The first that most people heard of his campaign was on Friday October 13 1307, when all knights present in the Templar houses in France were summarily arrested. The charges fell into two main categories: heresy and inappropriate sexual acts—usefully all-

encompassing offences, including:

> During the initiation of a knight, brothers were directed to deny Christ and spit on the cross.
>
> The knights adored and worshipped a cat or a head.
>
> During ceremonies they practised obscene kisses on mouth, navel and buttocks.
>
> The non-clerical officials of the Order heard confession and absolved brethren.
>
> The brothers encouraged sodomy between members.

Knights were imprisoned and in most cases cruelly tortured to extract confessions — one knight attended his trial carrying a bag of his own bones that had fallen from his feet as they were roasted during 'questioning'. Later, these confessions were retracted, even though the individuals concerned knew that this would condemn them to the stake as relapsed heretics. The Grand Master himself, Jacques de Molay, was to suffer this fate.

King Philip's hopes of replenishing his finances were to be dashed. Despite the sudden arrests, thorough searches of Templar properties and vicious torture, no 'treasure' was found, nor any indication of its whereabouts. Various theories have tried to account for this, the most prosaic being that the Templars' wealth was bound up in property and credit and at this stage they had no extraneous valuables. But some writers point to the fact that not much of anything was found—whether arms, horses or household effects—either in France or other countries. A silver reliquary was discovered at the Paris temple, but this was very much the exception.

Furthermore, Templars themselves were thinner on the ground than expected—in most properties scarcely more than a skeleton crew. Did this lack of men and possessions mean the Order was in decline, with most of its members getting older, and their preceptories in a state of disrepair, containing only a few basic items? Or did they have advance warning of the moves against them, and had taken steps to spirit their treasures away, never to be seen again?

And where were their ships? Most of the Templars' properties were sited close to navigable waterways so, if the knights had known of the impending arrests, it would not have been difficult for the fittest and most active members to slip away by boat and disappear until it was safe to return. Not that the remaining knights would have lacked confidence in their ability to defend themselves against the absurd charges. In fact, when arrested, they offered no resistance to the men taking them into custody.

In any case, it was only in France that the Templars were suppressed in such a vigorous and thorough manner. Other European rulers had been unwilling to go along with the wishes of the French king or, more expressly, the French Pope, and made no more than token moves to comply with instructions, using little or no torture. Significantly, in countries where torture was not used, the Templars made no confessions and were effectively freed. And they were prepared to stand up for themselves — in Germany, in May 1310, they showed up at the Council of Mainz in full armour and declared their innocence, offering to fight anyone who disagreed. The Council could find no fault and the knights left unmolested.

The Order was officially dissolved by the Pope in 1312. Two years later, the last Grand Master of the Order, Jacques de Molay, was burnt at the stake along with the Master of Normandy, Geoffroi de Charney. According to Charles Addison, de Molay's last words were:

> To say that which is untrue is a crime both in the sight of God and man. Not one of us has betrayed his God or his country. I do confess my guilt, which consists in having, to my shame and dishonour, suffered myself, through the pain of torture and the fear of death, to give utterance to falsehoods imputing scandalous sins and iniquities to an illustrious Order, which hath nobly served the cause of Christianity. I disdain to seek a wretched and disgraceful existence by engrafting another lie upon the original falsehood.

Legend has it that de Molay said he would meet Philip and Pope Clement in the afterlife, within the year — and sure enough both king and pope were dead before the year was over.

Above A portrait of Jacques de Molay who, having joined the Order aged twenty-one, rose to become the 23rd and last Grand Master of the Knights Templar.
Left In 1314 de Molay was sentenced to be burned at the stake for heresy. The picture illustrates the legend that de Molay was led to his death shouting that King Philip and Pope Clement would 'face a tribunal with God' within a year.

✛ POPE CLEMENT specified that after the suppression of the Order in 1312, all Templar properties throughout Europe should be passed on to the Knights Hospitaller. This meant that the possessions of the Order would remain under Church control and not fall into the hands of secular rulers. And it now seems that the Pope wished all along to distance himself from King Philip's suppression. Centuries later, in 2001, the so-called 'Chinon parchment' was unearthed from Vatican archives, casting a new light on Clement's apparent collusion. He had managed to question the Templars held at Chinon Castle in 1308, after which he privately pardoned the Order with the statement, 'We hereby decree that they are absolved by the Church and may again receive Christian sacraments.'

Yet Jacques de Molay was burnt in 1314—six years was evidently not long enough to implement the Pope's intention. He must have been totally compromised by Philip, unable to broadcast what he knew—Clement's private pardon may have had more to do with easing his own conscience and saving his own soul than keeping de Molay from the flames.

Elsewhere, the Templars faced mixed fortunes. In England, after 1312, members of the Order who had been arrested were released after admitting some minor errors and doing penance, and allowed to join other monastic orders. Many Templars had fled the initial arrests in France and England and made their way to neutral countries such as Scotland, Ireland and Portugal, there to live as best they could.

Perhaps the final word on their history belongs to two old Templars in the Holy Land, whose story is quoted in Malcolm Barber's *The New Knighthood*. One Ludolph of Sudheim, a German priest, was on pilgrimage in about 1340 when he met two elderly men on the shores of the Dead Sea.

> He discovered that they were former Templars, captured when the city of Acre had fallen to the Mamluks in May 1291, who had since then been living in the mountains, cut off from all communication with Latin Christendom. They had wives and children and had survived by working in the sultan's service; they had no idea that the Order of the Temple had been suppressed in 1312 and that the Grand Master had been burnt to death as a relapsed heretic two years later.

The men were eventually repatriated, with their families, and were allowed to live out the remainder of their existence in peace.

> These two Templars were the almost forgotten remnants of what, barely a generation before, had appeared to be one of the most powerful monastic orders in Christendom. During the thirteenth century the Order may have had as many as 7,000 knights, sergeants and serving brothers, and priests, while its associate members, pensioners, officials, and subjects numbered many times that figure. By about 1300 it had built a network of at least 870 castles, preceptories, and subsidiary houses, examples of which could be found in almost every country in western Christendom.

The history of the Templars was never going to be a universally agreed account of their rise and fall. Their shadowy beginnings are muddied further

IN SEARCH OF THE KNIGHTS TEMPLAR

by partial early chronicles, while their meteoric rise to power and wealth generated as much resentment and suspicion as admiration, and their shockingly abrupt end lent itself again to the verdict of parties who had their own agenda. Essentially, the Templar story could be told any way according to motive and imagination.

THE TEMPLARS IN IMAGINATION

Centuries before *The Da Vinci Code* phenomenon that linked the Templars to ancient mysteries, they had a presence in medieval romances and morality tales. The Italian poet Dante—a herald of the Renaissance—features them, in his masterpiece *The Divine Comedy*, an account of a journey through hell, purgatory and heaven. He completed this epic work in 1321, while memories of the Templars' suffering were still fresh; he sympathised with them, as being the victims of the greed of the French king. Dante is the first example of how anti-establishment, progressive artists in history have tended to cite the case

Below A typical late-Romantic depiction of the lone weary Templar knight returning from the Crusades, by the German painter Karl Friedrich Lessing.

Above 'Turn, False Hearted Templar! Let Go Her Whom Thou Art Unworthy to Touch!' from *Ivanhoe* by Sir Walter Scott. This particular illustration is taken from *Ivanhoe For Boys and Girls*, published in 1924.

of the Templars as a way of illustrating the failures of Church or government.

A work rather more accessible to public taste today appeared some four hundred years later, in the shape of Sir Walter Scott's *Ivanhoe* (1819). Scott portrayed his Templar character Brian de Bois Guilbert as arrogant and high-handed. The model was probably Brian de Jay, the English Grand Master who swore fealty to King Edward I and fought against the Scots — both of which actions were completely against the principles of the Order. The historical Brian was killed at the Battle of Falkirk, but not before he had managed to make himself very unpopular. Scott's characterisation was highly influential, and it is possible to see the image he gives to the Order reflected in some of the assumptions made by historians, such as the Reverend Oliver in 1841 when he was excavating at Temple Bruer (see page 157).

While Scott is acknowledged as the creator of the historical novel, blending realism with adventure and romance, the later writer H. Rider Haggard also drew on tradition and legend, to great effect. Better known for his *King Solomon's Mines* and *She*, he wrote *Red Eve* in 1911, a tale set in Edward III's reign. One of the characters is an ex-Templar knight who continues to live around his former home, the preceptory of Dunwich, described thus:

> It was a very great chamber where, before their order was dispersed, all the Knights Templar had been wont to dine with those who visited them at times of festival. Tattered banners still hung among the cobwebs of the ancient roof, the shields of past masters with stately blazonings were carved in stone upon the walls. But of all this departed splendour but little could be seen, since the place was lit only by a single lamp of whale's oil and a fire that burned upon the wide stone hearth.

Dunwich was also the probable inspiration for the setting of a story by M. R. James, 'Oh, Whistle, and I'll Come to You, My Lad' (1904). Here, a Cambridge professor decides to get away from it all in a small guest house on the Norfolk coast. While there, the professor takes a walk along the sea:

> He must, he quite rightly concluded, be on the site of the preceptory he had promised to look at. It seemed not unlikely to reward the spade of the explorer; enough of the foundations was probably left at no great depth to throw a good deal of light on the general plan. He remembered vaguely that the Templars, to whom this site had belonged, were in the habit of building round churches, and he thought a particular series of the humps or mounds near him did appear to be arranged in something of a circular form.

The story builds on a gradual sense of menace that originates from an antique whistle found at the Templars' church. Dunwich itself was the known site of a preceptory. The town is a victim of coastal erosion, and has gradually

IN SEARCH OF THE KNIGHTS TEMPLAR

been slipping into the sea for centuries. It has always had an eerie reputation; as churches disappeared into the sea, coffins stuck out from the cliffs before falling on to the rocks below.

The Knights Templar legacy also features rather more substantially in Lawrence Durrell's *The Avignon Quintet* (1974–85), its ruins and mystery a counterpart to modern times in southern France.

One book could be said to have initiated the modern preoccupation with ancient biblical legends involving the Templars: *The Holy Blood and the Holy Grail* by Michael Baigent,

Above An early nineteenth-century representation of the Order by Francis Phillip Stephanoff, entitled *The Crusader*. A stricken knight is surrounded by his fellows as a shackled infidel prisoner lies to one side.

Richard Leigh and Henry Lincoln. This in turn had been brought about by Lincoln's casual purchase in 1969 of a paperback published some years earlier in France: *Le trésor maudit* ('The Accursed Treasure') by Gérard de Sède. This book tells the story of how a poor parish priest in the south of France, Beringer Saunier, suddenly gained wealth and started to build strange buildings around his home village of Rennes-le-Château. Many of the buildings contained occult symbolism.

Intrigued, Henry Lincoln was eventually able to investigate the mystery through three *Chronicle* programmes for BBC Television, which among other revelations returned the Templars to the mythical role of guardians of the Grail. They are given an esoteric mission, which restates their function in Jerusalem. Far from being an order created by nine knights to protect pilgrims, their mission was one planned years before and was primarily to do with gaining access to the Temple Mount, which they did by being granted the site of the al-Aqsa mosque when they were founded. They needed access in order to look for holy relics.

With Baigent and Leigh, Lincoln published *The Holy Blood and the Holy Grail* in 1982, expanding on the BBC programmes and including details of the secret order, the 'Priory of Sion'. The book suggests that the Templars were in fact party to a secret, protected since the time of Christ: Christ and Mary Magdalene were lovers, if not man and wife, and they produced at least one child who was spirited away to France. This was the secret that the priest in Rennes discovered after finding parchments hidden in his church during restoration. This union created a bloodline from Christ with the descendants being protected through history. It is suggested that Grand Masters of the Priory of Sion are part of the bloodline, and include Da Vinci and Isaac Newton among other notables.

This bloodline is in fact the real Holy Grail. In French the Holy Grail is spelt '*San Grael*'; this should actually be spelt '*Sang Real*' — 'royal blood'. Near Rennes le Château, there are legends of Mary Magdalene arriving by boat to begin a new life, and bringing a 'secret' with her.

Dan Brown's bestselling *The Da Vinci Code* picks up on this notion, also incorporating theories put forward by Lynn Picknett and Clive Prince in their 1997 book *The Templar Revelation*. Brown cleverly works all the salient points of the Rennes-le-Château / Priory of Sion mystery into a pacy romp. This is an effective device as it allows the mystery to unfold incrementally.

Some years before these books exploded on to the market, Umberto Eco had played with the idea of mystic mysteries in his *Foucault's Pendulum* (1989), parodying the world of the historical conspiracy theory, including the famous notion that a man who is mad will eventually start talking about the Templars.

Templars have also featured on screen. Apart from various versions of the evergreen *Ivanhoe* (the early TV series starred a very young Roger Moore in the title role), Templars have a role in *Revelation*, a watchable British film of 2001. This puts them firmly in their 'Holy Blood/Holy Grail' role as guardians of a holy relic, this time called the 'loculus'. Terence Stamp is the master of a Templar-like order that has turned nasty...

An altogether more serious take on the historical role of the Templars features in Ridley Scott's 2005 film, *Kingdom of Heaven*. Despite a few flaws, this film is in fact the best ever made regarding the Crusades.

What is unfortunately not authentic is the depiction of the Templars as inflexible warmongers. At the time the film is set there were divisions among the crusaders, and maniacs such as Reynard de Chatillon were using the Order for their own purposes, but integration with the local population was

IN SEARCH OF THE KNIGHTS TEMPLAR

something the Templars initiated and they were generally the least bellicose of the factions in the kingdom. That aside, though, the film gives a realistic depiction of the Holy Land and Jerusalem at this time—the battle scenes, the weapons, the buildings, and how people dressed and lived. As Robert Fisk reported in *The Independent*, it was well received by Middle Eastern filmgoers, who appreciated not only the Muslim characters being played by Muslim actors, but the whole portrayal of the merciful nature of Islam.

Meanwhile, this partial overview of Templars in the imagination can always be augmented by the internet—along with, of course, factually based history. A rising number of sites attest to the growing interest in the Order, disseminating a huge amount of information, from sober analysis to lunatic fringe theorising and everything in between.

No doubt Templars will go on featuring on the page, on the screen and on the web: a testament to their enduring hold on the popular imagination — which in many cases is fired by their own tangible legacy in the landscape: their buildings, and the often strange decorations that reinforce their aura of mystery.

TEMPLAR ARCHITECTURE AND SYMBOLISM

The Templars brought to their building works the discipline, efficiency and pragmatism they displayed on the battlefield. As members of an international organisation, they could benefit from the expertise and technical knowledge of different countries' building traditions, particularly those of England, France and Italy. Furthermore, with their openness to new ideas, they would observe and adapt the style and techniques of sophisticated Muslim architects in the East.

Opposite and left Krak des Chevaliers, which was built by the Hospitallers, remains the finest example of the castles built by the military orders to defend the Holy Land.

Initially, at least, form would follow function, and depended on the environment in which the Templars were operating. Where they were militarily active, such as in Palestine and the Iberian peninsula, they built defensively — which meant castles, often on a massive scale. They would usually employ local labour, or prisoners if they were available. The ruins of the castles of the military orders still survive in the Middle East, for example at Athlit, and in Syria the mighty Krak des Chevaliers.

In Europe, they would also think defensively where there was a chance they might face enemies, constructing fortified manors. In a peaceful environment their buildings reflected local needs, whether barns and granaries for agriculture, forges and mills for industry, or warehouses for maritime trading. Templar headquarters would also need to accommodate administrative offices.

The Templars' preceptories reflected both their religious observance and their secular enterprise, being a cross between a monastery and a medieval manor. With their close links to the Cistercians and Bernard of Clairvaux, they would have had a pattern on which to build, including church, cloisters, hall, dormitories, kitchens and a range of outbuildings. Being a military order, the Templars also needed extensive stables and a place for exercising their horses, as well as for training in arms.

Their style of building reflected their functional role; they were also influenced by the austere Bernard of Clairvaux, who, as well as disdaining the flamboyance of the secular knights, abhorred excess of any kind. Just as monastic life should be simple and frugal, so monastic building should be plain, with no unnecessary ornamentation. (Bernard lived by his own ethic — when younger, he inhabited a room the size of a cupboard for approximately a decade, with a roof so low that he couldn't stand upright.)

While the Templars adopted this kind of early Puritanism, their estates were emphatically commercial: not only did they have to sustain the members of the Order, they also had to generate substantial profits to send back to the Holy Land.

Relatively few of the Templars' non-religious buildings can still be seen today. One striking example is at Cressing Temple in Essex (see page 86), where the huge wooden barns have survived for nearly a thousand years despite the ravages of weather and the danger of fire — a testament to the quality of workmanship the Templars insisted on. What usually survive are their places of worship, perhaps because they were mainly constructed in stone, on a more substantial scale than other buildings in the complex. And being on consecrated ground would have given them a measure of protection.

Below The round church of St John in Little Maplestead in Essex, England. A surviving example of the small round church favoured by early Templars and Hospitallers.

IN SEARCH OF THE KNIGHTS TEMPLAR

While the external appearance of these surviving Templar churches may not be too different from the original, the interior, like that of other Norman buildings both secular and religious, differs in one striking respect. The austere grey stones of today would have been glowing with bright colours and decorations, hung with banners and often carpeted—a rich feast for the eye as relays of priests sang perpetual masses and incense infused the air.

The Templars' 'round churches', constructed on a circular plan, can be found throughout Europe — not every such medieval church was built by the Order, but probably most of them. The reason for the circular design is unclear; most writers agree that the Holy Sepulchre in Jerusalem was the model, but others have pointed to the octagonal Dome of the Rock close to their headquarters at the Temple Mount, also used on Templar seals.

Perhaps there was a greater significance, beyond the three-dimensional. On early medieval Christian maps the Holy Sepulchre was shown as the centre of the world. The round church could be seen as an imitation, a magical re-creation of the tomb of Christ.

In another interpretation, the circular design allowed knights to be seated around the perimeter in a kind of visual democracy — no one man could sit at the head—which may have been a reflection of the 'all for one' spirit of the Templars. There may also be echoes of the legends of the Arthurian round table with which the Templars would have been familiar. Whatever the connotations, the enduring appeal of the circle symbol had been tangible in the landscape for thousands of years, and still is — in the form of great stone monuments such as Stonehenge, the purpose of which can only be guessed at.

The structure of buildings may therefore embody layers of meaning, decipherable to those acquainted with symbol and story. Certainly the

Templars, men of their time in a deeply spiritual—or superstitious—age, not only incorporated significance into the fabric of their buildings; they also left tangible evidence in carvings and other decorations, many of which seem strangely at odds with their Christian ethic.

✠ WHERE THE TEMPLARS did accord with mainstream Christian thought was in the veneration of holy relics, which were seen as having enormous, tangible power, touched as they were by the divine. Fragments of the True Cross, bones of saints, garments worn by the blessed — possession of such sacred objects could bring God on your side.

Competition for relics was intense. A venerable skeleton could be pulled apart as individuals fought for possession. When Hugh, Bishop of Lincoln in the later twelfth century (later St Hugh), was presented with bones attributed to Mary Magdalene, he just had to possess a piece, promptly grabbing a finger and taking a bite. He explained his rash action by noting that if indeed he was being blasphemous he would have been 'struck down'!

Famous relics would attract a multitude of pilgrims to a shrine or church. Sometimes these relics were on permanent show, where the faithful could readily adore them, or locked away in richly decorated reliquaries to be brought out on special occasions. Crusaders would be especially keen to possess their own relics, their very presence in the Holy Land being to rescue holy sites from the Muslims. The Templars' ambitions in this direction led to the most contentious claims made against them at their suppression. Their proximity to the Temple Mount, and their rumoured exploration of its tunnels and caves housing the holiest relics of all, associated them ever after with the Holy Grail and the Ark of the Covenant. Subsequent writers have been more or less polarised in their interpretation, some adhering firmly to the known academic history, others dwelling on the alleged occult side of the Order.

Above A holy relic, kept in the Templar church in Tomar, Portugal.
Opposite above The enigmatic seal of the Templars – 'TEMPLI SECRETUM' – depicting the pre-Christian Gnostic symbol of the Abraxas. Its specific use and meaning are uncertain.
Opposite below A statue of St Anne, the mother of the Virgin, in the dress of an Egyptian priestess, holding the Virgin and Christ. This statue is said to have been brought back from the Holy Land to Tomar, Portugal, by the Templars.

Certainly the Templars' contemporaries were ready to tar them with heresy. While living and fighting in the East, the knights would have encountered some of the Christian sects, such as Manicheans and Gnostics, who were active there. These sects had been existing in isolation, separated from the western Church after the Muslim incursion. While the western Church, centred on Rome, had been energetically standardising its teachings and distilling the New Testament down to a consistent doctrine, the eastern sects had remained unaffected, persisting in their own interpretations. Consequently, by the time crusaders and western clergy entered the Holy Land, the beliefs of these eastern sects were markedly different from Roman orthodoxy and thus heretical.

The Templars' readiness to adapt to local people and customs made them

IN SEARCH OF THE KNIGHTS TEMPLAR

automatically suspect. They fuelled suspicion by incorporating some Gnostic symbols into their seals, such as the Abraxas. Whether this was purely decorative or a statement of belief is unclear.

Some writers have suggested that the Templars were influenced by the 'Johannite heresy', a belief that John the Baptist was the true Messiah. The Order certainly did revere this saint, but it is unlikely they placed him above Christ.

The Templars also employed symbols on their seals and in their buildings that were not so much discredited Christian but openly pagan, drawing on magical symbols such as the pentagram, the 'green man' and a so-called 'head'. Templars were accused at their trial of worshipping this 'head', and denied the charge; other witnesses in England claimed the knights were in possession of not only heads but other idols. The 'head' has sometimes been referred to as 'Baphomet', apparently a corruption of 'Mohammed', and its existence has no basis in fact.

At Templecombe in Somerset a painting of a face was discovered in the

Above left The identity of the figure portrayed on the Templecombe panel is unclear, though painted with great reverence; possibly John the Baptist or Christ. The similarity to the Turin Shroud is unmistakable.

Above right High above the altar at the eastern end of the Templar church of Santa Maria do Olival in Tomar, Portugal: the sign of Venus, the pentagram, also found on many of the Templars' gravestones in the area.

1950s. It is unusual in that it has no indication of divinity, no halo or symbol that would be appropriate for Christ or a saint; it is the head of an ordinary man, but painted in a manner that is clearly meant for reverence. The similarities between this head and that portrayed on the shroud of Turin, another relic the Templars were alleged to have held, are unmistakable.

Some Templar buildings make a feature of the octagonal shape and the number '8'. The reason for this is unknown; it may be a general stylistic tendency without any esoteric meaning. The symmetry of the number '8' does reflect the cross pattée with its eight corners, and of course the mosque on the Temple Mount has an octagonal structure. The number '8' can also be found represented in Templar grave slabs, piscinas, fonts and floor tiles.

One way that the Templars could literally leave their personal mark was in carvings, which are open to various interpretations. Explicitly religious images would give a devotional focus, especially when in captivity—as in Chinon and Lincoln castles—when the knights had no alternative.

Less formally, the knights would leave what can be called graffiti—the

IN SEARCH OF THE KNIGHTS TEMPLAR

appeal of leaving tangible evidence of one's presence is by no means a modern phenomenon. In common with other crusaders and pilgrims, they left carved markings in many of the places they visited, particularly holy sites. The medieval pilgrim trail ran through Europe, and at many points the travellers carved signs, usually to indicate they had been there and to say where they were going. The sign of the cross of Jerusalem would indicate a trip to the Holy Land.

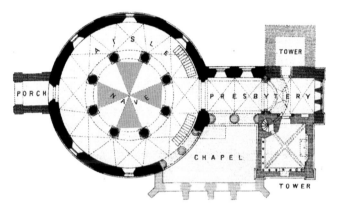

The study of medieval graffiti is a relatively neglected area of research. By its nature, graffiti is a spontaneous act, with no official record or note of the motivation behind it. For the Templars, who professed to be 'unlettered', perhaps symbols substituted for the written word.

The Templars left an indelible mark throughout Christendom, as much in commercial enterprise as in the buildings they constructed.

Top left A carving on a Templar grave in Portugal. The number '8' symbol has an early Möbius Strip running through it, the symbol of infinity.
Top right The hourglass '8' symbol in the south wall of a Templar church in Garway, Herefordshire.
Above A ground plan of a Templar round church, with its eight pillars. The Templars' cross pattée has been added to demonstrate how it integrates with the design.
Left Medieval graffiti from St Swithun's Church in Leadenham, Lincolnshire.

THE TEMPLARS IN EUROPE

After official papal approval was given in 1127 the Templars started to establish themselves throughout Europe and beyond. Over an area of thousands of square miles the Order maintained a disciplined and productive presence, from the wastes of the north to the shores of the Mediterranean, founding modest centres that would flourish as the Order's wealth grew.

Once established, the Templars' growth owes much to the monastic model as, borrowing particularly from the Cistercians (known as the 'monks of the frontier'), they would send missionaries to remote outposts to curry favour, and establish a foothold. Yet, while the Templars did situate centres in marginal areas of Europe they also placed great emphasis on securing sea ports and strategic points that would help achieve their stated aim of controlling and protecting the major international sites of pilgrimage. In facilitating the routes that would carry pilgrims to Jerusalem, Rome and beyond, the Order created an intricate web of communication networks. This helped the Templars to move beyond their original declared objective of protection towards the formation of a major military force.

It is worth bearing in mind that modern country borders, such as those of Spain and Portugal, did not exist in the early Middle Ages, and Europe was essentially a collection of kingdoms, each one a potential supporter for the military orders. England and France were the European centres, although the Order had a presence in the rest of Europe and outposts in eastern states such as Poland and Silesia as well as Cyprus and the Western Baltic region, modern-day Croatia. These two positions, on an island and along the Adriatic coast respectively, demonstrate how, just as in England, the Templars carefully positioned their centres. It was essential to have access to a major road or waterway to facilitate the rapid transport of men and resources, and buildings were erected according to location and function. These tended to fall into general categories: castles, hostels, hospitals, farms and religious buildings (chapels and churches built to serve the centre). When the Templars received land that could be used for agriculture, for example in Normandy, they established preceptories. Called commanderies in mainland Europe, these were a cross between a monastery and a medieval manor, designed to realise the maximum profit from the surrounding land. The commandery would act as an administrative centre for the Templars' activities and properties in a given area, though it itself would remain ultimately under the control of the Order's country headquarters.

Beyond this, Paris was essentially the main office for the European provinces, working in tandem with the headquarters in Jerusalem. The Order also had houses at most of the major ports, for example Bristol, Wexford in Ireland, and along the east coast of France at Les Bias, Les Epaux and their principal port, La Rochelle. From these they could trade throughout the Mediterranean and beyond, and it has been suggested that from the heavily

Above The octagonal rotunda, known as the Charola of the convent of Christ: the magnificent headquarters of the Knights Templar in Portugal.

fortified harbour at La Rochelle they launched trading missions, not only to the British Isles, but also to Greenland and the North American mainland. Defensive castles were built where there was a risk of attack. Houses that could act as hostelries were founded along established overland routes such as the area between Bordeaux and Marseille, used to avoid the hazardous sea voyage around the Iberian Peninsula. From this strong base the Templars could service their twin aims of pilgrimage and protection.

At their height the Templars were in the forefront of many aspects of European culture: acting as negotiators for kings, international bankers, pioneer traders and farmers. By the time of their decline many of these occupations had slipped from their control. Other factions had taken over the Templars' role; the Jews had taken the banking, the Italians the trade. It was a shift that left the Order increasingly isolated. They were further weakened when they declined the opportunity to merge with the Hospitallers and stuck resolutely to their original aim of securing the Holy Land as a Christian state.

While Britain is often regarded as the area in which the Templars were able to expand most successfully both fiscally and agriculturally, perhaps the best-known Templar area in Europe today is the Languedoc (literally meaning the tongue – *langue* – of the Oc) in southern France. The ruins of Templar castles remain dotted around the mountains of this landscape and it was here that the Templars were said to have planned to establish their own state in a region that was familiar with the crusading principle. It was here in the early thirteenth century that the Cathars were brutally massacred and effectively wiped out. Any mass dissident movement perceived to pose a very real threat to the Vatican was put to the sword rather than allow any potential sympathisers to escape. Today the crusade against the Cathars is often viewed as the hysterical suppression of a sect, yet politically a whole region of France appeared to be moving away from the rule of the Church, and the loss of control and tax revenue prompted swift action. The Inquisition was founded during this period as a tool with which to assess the level of heresy through interrogation. The Templars would later face the same brutal treatment.

The powerbase the Templars maintained in the Languedoc can be seen

Right and Opposite
Two examples of the house markers of the military Orders. The Knights of Christ in Idanha a Velha, Portugal (right), and (opposite) a Templar marker from Leeds.

IN SEARCH OF THE KNIGHTS TEMPLAR

from the many villages and towns they founded to provide support and labour for preceptories and castles. La Couvertoirade and Collioure are just two of the villages which continue to acknowledge their Templar founders. In Portugal too, the Templar headquarters of Tomar is today a busy centre that celebrates its knightly origins. The same cannot be said for Baldock in England, where the Templars are all but forgotten, their only visible legacy the particular grid pattern of the streets of the town centre.

In the towns and villages the Templars and other orders marked their properties with distinctive crosses to display ownership and tax exemption. That they paid no local taxes was only one of the reasons that the Templars were able to amass their great wealth in Europe. They were a disciplined group who committed themselves to the sole purpose of generating funds for the Holy Land. They were unique in the trust they engendered; vast sums of money were deposited with them; and they received donations of land and money throughout the Continent. Each Templar house, church or castle had the effect of raising the Order's local profile, and very rapidly they had an infrastructure that was able to receive donations, process international financial transactions and generate wealth to support its campaigns.

Yet despite this, and for all the properties the order oversaw throughout Europe, the artefacts that were recovered after the arrests were scant. This has led to the suggestion that the Templars had prior knowledge of moves against them and took the precaution of sending what valuables they had to safety in other regions, a notion that has led to much speculation about where the Templars might have hidden their 'treasure'. An entire fleet of Templar ships vanished from La Rochelle on 13 October 1307, seven years prior to the death of de Molay, and its destination has never been known. Perhaps the most imaginative theory concerns Oak Island off Nova Scotia. Here, in 1795, a 'well' was found, which descended at least 200 feet into the earth and contained a number of traps and defences to prevent access to whatever was at the bottom. This soon led to the conclusion among some writers that the only organisation with the resources to create such an elaborate hiding place was the Templars. Despite numerous attempts using a variety of technologies, the well has so far maintained its secrets, and the supposed Templar treasure is no closer to being discovered today than at the time of their demise.

Europe and the Holy Land at the time of the Templars

THE MAP shows some of the more significant Templar sites, but by no means all, and a fraction of the thousands of properties they controlled. Their presence stretched from the borders of Christendom on the Iberian peninsula to the northern states of the Baltic region. The crusader states are shown roughly as they stood at the founding of the Templars in 1118.

THE FOUNDERS of the Templars all came from the Champagne region of France just south of Paris. They shared the lands with the other military orders: the Hospitallers, who had properties throughout Europe; and the Teutonic Knights, who were based to the north with their home town at Marienburg, from where they would engage in the Baltic Crusades

against the pagan tribes. Also marked are general routes taken during the Crusades. Once the Kingdom of Jerusalem was established, these routes would have functioned as the supply lines for troops and resources to support the Christian presence in the Holy Land.

The Templars also traded throughout the Mediterranean, and from the eastern ports in Britain with the countries to the north in the Hanseatic League.

THE TEMPLARS briefly held the island of Cyprus, which continued to play an important role after the loss of the Holy Land, when crusaders based their king and government there. After they were arrested on Cyprus, the Templars were held in Kyrenia Castle.

Denmark

HANSEATIC LEAGUE

TEMPELBURG

MARIENBURG
HQ Teutonic Knights

Frisia

Poland

RUSSIAN PRINCIPALITIES

◉ COLOGNE

TEMPLESTEIN

METZ

WESTERN

EMPIRE

Austria

◉ VIENNA

Hungary

KHANATE OF THE GOLDEN HORDE

ON

VERONA

BOLOGNA

VRANA

Serbia

NICE   LUCCA

KLISS

MARSEILLE

Papal

BYZANTINE

LLIOURE   Elba   *States*

EMPIRE

Corsica   ◉ ROME

SAN LEONARDO

CONSTANTINOPLE ◉

BARI

Sardinia   TARENT

Kingdom

of

Sicily

PALERMO

Rhodes

KYRENIA

◉ ◉

Cyprus

CRUSADE
STATES

Crete   FAMAGUSTA

◉ DAMASCUS

ACRE

JERUSALEM

Christian (Catholic) territory

Other Christian territory

Muslim territory

Mongol territory

Other

⊕ Templar site

◉ Major medieval centre

} Broadly defined routes taken by
Crusaders

THE TEMPLARS IN BRITAIN

That first well-received visit to England by Hugh de Payens after the Council of Troyes (see page 17) was the start of a close relationship between the Templars and the lands across the Channel — one that outlived the duration of the Order itself. While rulers and other powerful landowners throughout Christendom showered donations of land and valuables on the Order, conventionally as a kind of spiritual insurance, England was particularly generous. Of course, the Norman nobility was in a position to do this; having invaded England barely sixty years earlier, they had a lot of formerly Saxon land to give away.

The first recorded land given to the Templars is at Cressing Temple in Essex, donated by Matilda, the wife of King Stephen, in 1137. This may not have been the first actual Templar property — records of other donations may have been lost. The first record of property donated in London dates from 1144, though at least one authority in the early twentieth century (the *Catholic Encyclopedia*) states that it was 1118, the same date as their founding.

It is clear that many dates cannot be relied upon for theories about their expansion. Some authors have suggested a diffusionist London-centric model with the Order spreading out gradually through the countryside. But it is more likely that a number of modest bases were set up at the same time, and then gradually grew in land and wealth, particularly along the eastern side of England.

Lincolnshire and Yorkshire were to become the most productive areas for the Templars. Both were dominated by their respective capital cities, at this time major ecclesiastic powers rivalling London. Having been important Roman centres, they had an existing infrastructure of roads; they were also ports, with links to the major markets and fairs of Flanders, France and the Hanseatic countries in northern Europe. They were surrounded by many

Below An early twentieth-century stereogram of Ludlow 'Templar' chapel showing the building in a ruinous state. It has now been lightly repaired.

624. Ludlow Knight's Templar Chapel.

IN SEARCH OF THE KNIGHTS TEMPLAR

acres of land that were made available to the Order — here, and throughout the eastern counties, the Templars were to create one of the largest and most efficient agricultural enterprises ever seen.

The trademark of the Templars was in developing the natural resources of the land, whatever they might be. As well as staple crops and livestock, they built up such endeavours as tin mining in Cornwall, horse breeding in Ireland, and vineyards in the south of England (and of course elsewhere in Europe — the French wine Châteauneuf du Pape was a Templar creation).

Some of the Templars' new land came complete with existing settlements; others, especially in less productive or popular parts, required a village to be built to accommodate their labourers. In time the Templars became major landowners themselves, embedded deep into the local life and economy — to such an extent that their name has survived in English placenames for centuries: Temple Bruer, Temple Hirst, and so on.

Few fit knights would have resided for long in their preceptories, either in Britain or mainland Europe. Their main purpose was to fight in the Holy Land, along with their sergeants and squires, often being called upon to undertake more than one tour of duty. So most of the Templars resident in preceptories would be new recruits in training, or perhaps those veteran crusaders brought back to recuperate from wounds. The estates would be worked by lay labour — though to stringent standards set by the Templars; just as the knights themselves supplied military muscle, so their estates would generate as much profit as possible to be sent back east for the war effort.

Above The 'Jew's house' in Lincoln was owned by the Templars and leased to Aaron the Jew in 1158. The leasing of property was a way in which the Templars were able to maintain control and gain profit from property donated to them.

While ensuring that their estates were run profitably, the Templars did not neglect their spiritual needs, incorporating churches and chapels in their settlements. They built eight known 'round churches' in Britain: one each at Garway, Dover, Hereford, Bristol, Aslackby and Temple Bruer, and two in London. There are some others occasionally claimed as Templar churches, including Ludlow Castle's Mary Magdalene Chapel, Cambridge's Holy Sepulchre, Northampton's Holy Sepulchre, and Little Maplestead's St John's. Of these, it is possible that Cambridge and Ludlow were Templar but later sold off, or given away, before 1185. Northampton was built by a crusader, but not a Templar, and Little Maplestead was actually Hospitaller.

The confusion between Templar and Hospitaller property is understandable, given their similarities — and it is compounded by the fact that the Hospitallers were given all the Templars' lands and property in 1312 after the latter's dissolution. This meant that in areas with few records, the evidence for the presence of the Templars may have been lost.

Another source of confusion is the interchangeable names for what is effectively the monastic estate headquarters — known as either a preceptory or commandery. 'Preceptory' tends to be more common in Britain, generally applied to Templar and occasionally Hospitaller property. 'Commandery' is found throughout Europe where it applies equally to both Templars and Hospitallers, but in Britain it generally applies to Hospitallers only. So once the Hospitallers inherited the Templars' preceptories they in many cases changed the name to commandery.

The Hospitallers' own round churches include that at their headquarters in Clerkenwell, London, which was very similar to the Temple Church. And both were consecrated by the Patriarch of Jerusalem, Heraclius, at the same time, in 1185.

✝ THE TEMPLARS' TIES specifically to England were greatly strengthened by their close links to the Crown, from King Stephen onwards. As elsewhere on the Continent, they were often employed as advisers and given trusted positions outside the Order, such as treasurer or almoner, or acted as armed escort to the royals. Their independence meant that while they were not under the monarch's control, neither were they under anyone else's.

Their relationship with Stephen's successor, Henry II, was thrown into particular relief by the murder of Thomas Becket, the Archbishop of Canterbury. The guilty knights were ordered to do penance by donating land to the Templars and serving some years with the Order in the Holy Land. Their tombs remain today near the entrance to the al-Aqsa mosque, the Jerusalem headquarters of the Templars. Henry himself was ordered to do penance by going on a crusade. He agreed, but later managed to commute this to a donation and the foundation of a religious house.

The sword that killed Becket was included among the items logged as being on display at the London Temple when the English members were arrested in 1308.

The Becket legacy lives on even into modern times. In Watchet in Somerset, the Knights Templar School was opened in 1990, on land originally given to the Order by Reginald FitzUrse, one of the knights, in penance for his murderous deed.

Of Henry II's successors, the crusading Richard I was more at home in the Holy Land than in his own country. His brother John (according to Addison), when he in turn became king, 'frequently resided' at the London Temple — evidenced by the number of 'writs and precepts' to his 'lieutenants, sheriffs and bailiffs' he sent originating from there. At times he was in great need of Templar assistance. After he had refused to accept the papal appointment of Stephen Langton as Archbishop of Canterbury, he was excommunicated by Pope Innocent III, who then prompted the French king to plan an invasion of

England. In 1213 John travelled to the preceptory of Temple Ewell and, either there or in the small round chapel on the cliffs over Dover, pledged absolute fealty to the papal representative.

A couple of years later, Templars again featured in an iconic moment of English history: the Grand Master Aymeric was present at the signing of Magna Carta. Also present was William Marshal, the Earl of Pembroke, the famous knight later to be accepted into the Templars on his deathbed.

The Templars' relationship with the next king, Henry III, began badly when he complained about them to the Pope for appropriating houses and land that he felt belonged to him. It was not long, however, before the Templars were back in their role as peace makers with the king of France, and Henry apparently decided he would be buried in the Temple Church, presiding over the building of the new aisles in 1240. When he died, though, it was found he had changed his will and he was interred in Westminster Abbey.

Henry's successor, the ruthless expansionist Edward I, drew support from the Templar Grand Master Brian de Jay, memorably reincarnated in Scott's *Ivanhoe* (see page 28). It seems that de Jay, against all the principles of his Order, pledged fealty to the king and joined him in his fight against the Scots.

Above The substantial foundations of the round church at St Michael's Church in Garway, Herefordshire.

Edward II became king in 1307, the year that Philip of France orchestrated the suppression of the Templars. Edward's treatment of them could be seen as either sympathetic or weak. He resisted directions to have them arrested and dragged his heels when he was pressured to overrule common law and allow torture. He then allowed them to plead guilty to a minor charge and let them go, much to the chagrin of the French king.

✝ BY THE TIME of their suppression, the Knights Templar and their various enterprises had well and truly become part of the landscape of Britain. Throughout the country it is possible to see surviving evidence of their estates and industry, their churches and symbology. The next section follows in their footsteps.

THE SITES

THESE SITES GIVE THE CONTEXT OF THE TEMPLARS' LIFE in medieval Britain, both spiritual and secular: from churches great and small to manor houses and farm buildings — and rather less familiar evidence. The sites also represent a chronological picture of the Order: early preceptories growing in importance, becoming more substantial, and then in decline when, stripped of power, the knights could mark their presence only by carving the walls of their prisons.

FEW TANGIBLE remains are to be seen in Scotland: ancient ruins in Midlothian, and a vestigial chapel in Dumfries and Galloway, though the western seaboard carries memorials to legendary knights seeking refuge. And finally there is the one site that has captured the world's imagination— Rosslyn Chapel.

THE MIDLANDS (here including Cambridgeshire and Oxfordshire) encompasses the original church of a forest preceptory in Warwickshire; an original chapel in Leicestershire; traces of a preceptory in Oxfordshire; the sole surviving 'hospital', in Cambridgeshire, along with a neighbouring church; and an ancient church in Cambridge itself.

BEYOND ENGLISH BORDERS, the Templars did not settle much in Wales; just one of their churches remains, on the Gower. On the Borders, traces of one of their preceptories can be seen, in Herefordshire; while a tomb in Hereford Cathedral and a small chapel at Ludlow Castle have connections with the Order.

IN THE WILD SOUTHWEST, a stretch of Cornish moor was named after the Templars, and their church there given new life. Another of their churches lies in Bristol, this time in ruins, while a Somerset church houses one of their most evocative images: a 'head'.

TWO COUNTIES are singled out, to reflect their importance to the Templars: Yorkshire and Lincolnshire.

IN YORKSHIRE, traces of three preceptories survive, while a Victorian church houses poignant reminders of their presence in the county—which ended in the confines of York Castle.

TRACES OF ONLY ONE LINCOLNSHIRE preceptory remain, but two others can be theoretically reconstructed; a church holds an important single effigy; the castle and cathedral in Lincoln saw the Templars' imprisonment and trial, while one of their ancient inns in the city still carries on the same trade.

LONDON has the best-known site in the country, Temple Church, though another church houses a Templar altar, and the Tower holds an echo of their imprisonment.

IN THE SOUTHEAST, there are three Templar settlements in Kent, all linked to the important port of Dover; three notable churches, two in West Sussex and one in Hampshire; a surviving manor house in Berkshire; and two huge barns in Essex. A last site in the Southeast, in Hertfordshire, is one of the enduring mysteries: a cave.

KILMARTIN

KILMORY

ROSSLYN   TEMPLE

MOFFAT

WESTERDALE

PENHILL

RIBSTON   YORK

TEMPLE HIRST

LINCOLN
TEMPLE BRUER

GRANTHAM   ASLACKBY
ROTHLEY
SOUTH WITHAM

LUDLOW   TEMPLE BALSALL

DENNY
CAMBRIDGE

GARWAY   HEREFORD   ROYSTON

LLANMADOC   SANDFORD   LONDON   CRESSING
BISHAM   STROOD

BRISTOL   TEMPLE EWELL

TEMPLECOMBE   SELBORNE   SHIPLEY   DOVER
SOMPTING

TEMPLE

LONDON

THE TEMPLARS established themselves in London some time after the visit in 1128 of their founder Hugh de Payens, when he received donations from 'all good men'. In fact, as the generosity of wealthy patrons included the grants of various properties in the capital, the Templars needed to do little building here themselves — essentially just their preceptories. ✛ They built their first preceptory in what is now Holborn, standing at the current junction of Chancery Lane and High Holborn. This settlement included a round church, domestic buildings and outlying barns, along with a watermill that was powered by the River Fleet. The Order was then granted land a short distance to the south, near the banks of the Thames — which would have facilitated trade and the regular export of men and goods to the Holy Land — and shifted its whole enterprise there. ✛ For a while the Templars used both old and new preceptories, men, horses and wagons shuttling between them through the fields and in the process stamping out a new road — now known as Chancery Lane. The old temple was eventually sold to the Bishop of Lincoln for £66 13s 4d. ✛ Their new site is called the 'Temple' to this day, now a major centre of the legal profession; though Temple Church is the only remaining Templar building in the capital, their presence is echoed in such names as Temple Quay and Temple Pier — even Temple Underground station. ✛ The Templars' final contact with the capital had a poignant twist when the knights who had been arrested were brought from the provinces to the Tower of London. They were to make their public defence against the charges in the church of All Hallows by the Tower, whose original crypt still houses the altar brought from the round chapel in Athlit Castle: a monument to the Templars' last days in the Holy Land. ✜

✝ ALL HALLOWS BY THE TOWER

At its heart the oldest church in the city, All Hallows stands on Tower Hill, a site long associated with pagan influences and mysticism. Directly west of the Tower of London, and very close to it, the church was often touched by its bloody history, receiving the bodies of those executed as enemies of the state. When the Templars themselves were arrested, they defended themselves in All Hallows, fighting for their very existence. Although the fabric of the church is much changed today, the crypt is original, and contains a Templar altar.

Previous page *Agnus Dei*, the 'Lamb of God', found in the precincts of Temple Church. The sign of St John the Baptist, it is commonly associated with the Knights Templar.

Below left All Hallows from the south. The church was rebuilt after the Blitz, but retains its original Saxon crypt and the altar brought back by the Templars from the Holy Land. It was here that the upper ranks of the Order in England chose to defend themselves against the charges levelled at them.

Below right Samuel Pepys watched the Great Fire of London from the original spire. The striking copper-covered green spire seen here was added during the reconstruction.

The original church dates from Saxon times, being founded in the late seventh century by the Abbey of Barking — the church was long known as All Hallows Barking. There are still traces of that first church, in the undercroft with its three subterranean chapels. Part of a Roman pavement has also been found there, showing that this site has been occupied for at least two thousand years.

Tower Hill is closely associated with the ancient Celtic hero Bran the Blessed. According to legend, his severed head was brought here from the Irish battlefield on which he died; his followers buried it facing France, to guard against invasion. Bran also has a place in the Arthurian legends, especially the Holy Grail, and is still revered by modern-day Druids who convene on the hill in his honour. The notion of the severed head leads irresistibly to the cult of head-worship, of which the Templars were accused at their trial (see page 24).

A more concrete relationship between Templars and All Hallows came after their arrest, when they were brought from the provinces to London and imprisoned in the Tower. It was in All Hallows that the assembled higher ranks of the Order would defend themselves against the outrageous charges brought against them.

On 29 April 1311, William de la More, the Master of the Temple in England, along with some of the senior members of the Order, were led across the fields from the Tower to the church. Here, in an attempt to tell the world once and for all that they were innocent, William read out a statement.

> We believe all that the holy church believes and teaches us, we declare that our religion is founded on the vows of obedience, poverty and chastity, and the aiding in the conquest of the holy land of Jerusalem ... And we firmly deny and contradict one and all of us, all many of heresy and evil doings, contrary to the faith of the holy church...

William pleaded that he and his brethren be treated like 'true children of the church', and called on other Christians to attest for them.

> And if in our examinations we have said or done anything wrong through ignorance of a word, since we are unlettered men, we are ready to suffer for the holy church like him who died for us on the blessed cross ... we pray that our examination may be read and heard before ourselves and all people, in the very language and words in which it was given to you and written down on paper.

Eventually an agreement was reached as a way of allowing the remaining Templars to leave prison and for the king, Edward II, to be seen to have taken some action. This took the form of a kind of plea-bargain, the Templars agreeing to admit to some relatively minor irregularities and being given a form of penance. The physically fit knights were taken to St Paul's to make a statement of guilt and appeal for readmission to the Church. Those less able were heard in All Hallows.

Before their suppression, Templars had brought back altar stones from Athlit Castle in Acre, their last stronghold in the Holy Land to fall to the Saracens. These stones now stand at the eastern end of the undercroft, directly under the present high altar: an enduring and fitting monument to the Templars' presence.

Long after the Order had faded into history, the church of All Hallows itself continued its part in the capital's life. It was where the

Below A Celtic head, from Carran Chapel in County Clare, Ireland. The cult of head worship has long been associated with Tower Hill, where according to legend the head of Bran the Blessed was buried.

bodies of executed 'traitors', brought from the nearby Tower, rested while awaiting burial. They included many once powerful figures who had fallen from grace, most famously Sir Thomas More and Archbishop Laud. More happily, baptisms and marriages also took place—including some with a particular reference to the USA: William Penn, founder of Pennsylvania, was baptised in the church in 1644 and educated in the schoolroom, while John Quincy Adams, in due course the sixth president, was married in All Hallows in 1797.

It was William Penn's father, Admiral Penn, who was to save the church during the Great Fire of London in 1666. The fire started in Pudding Lane, just a few hundred yards away, and Penn Snr successfully orchestrated the fire-fighting efforts. Samuel Pepys, who was living nearby, recorded Penn's good work in his famous diary — and he himself had a panoramic view of the fire from the church's steeple:

> ...and there saw the saddest sight of desolation that I ever saw. Everywhere great flames. Oyle cellars and brimstone and other things burning. I became afeared to stay there long; and therefore down again as fast as I could, the fire being spread as far as I could see it...

Above The altar from the Templars' chapel at Athlit, brought back from the Holy Land by the Order.
Below A Saxon cross found in the ruins of All Hallows after the Blitz. The inscription has been translated as 'werhere', which Peter Ackroyd in *London: The Biography* points out sounds like a declaration from the early settlers: 'We are here'.
Opposite above At their trial, the Templars were said to have a 'gilded head' hidden in London. This example, from the British Museum, is English and contemporaneous with the Templars, but its origin is unknown. The hollow head would have contained a sacred relic, such as a piece of the True Cross.
Opposite below The eight-pointed Templar cross displayed at the centre of the altar.

A little under three hundred years later, Hitler's bombs succeeded where the Great Fire had failed. In common with the Temple Church, All Hallows suffered immense damage during the Blitz. All the woodwork in the main church was destroyed (although the Grinling Gibbons-carved font cover survived), with just the tower and walls remaining. But rebuilding work started after the war and the church was rededicated in 1957.

The undercroft has been made into a small museum of curiosities, which include a Saxon cross found in the church after the bombing, and the crow's nest from the ship that Ernest Shackleton took to the Arctic. (Being so near the Thames, that great artery of trade and traffic, All Hallows has long had a close association with all things maritime.) Another attraction for the general visitor is a brass-rubbing centre, with its facsimile medieval memorial brasses. Of the genuine medieval presence of the Templars, there is just the stone altar in the undercroft.

✝ TEMPLE CHURCH

In the heart of the city but a world away from its clamour and bustle, Temple Church lies secluded in an enclave of period buildings, courtyards and gardens, where even the pavements are testaments to history — their inset tombstones engraved with the names of the illustrious dead and their eulogies. During the working day this area is devoted to the workings of the legal profession but, when offices close, an atmosphere of peace and tranquillity settles down again, a more fitting evocation of the Templars' one-time spiritual headquarters.

The Templars' new round church was built on a magnificent scale to match the growing importance and wealth of the Order in England. Linked to the church was a range of grand buildings, complete with great hall, to accommodate the Master and his knights, their chaplains and retainers, while kitchens, fishponds and stables met their other needs. Spacious grounds stretched down to the Thames, providing areas for training and recreation.

The original church was without the large chancel seen today (the rectangular section built eastwards). The altar stands at the end of the chancel. The original church consisted of the round nave and either no chancel or a very much smaller version

The church was consecrated in 1185 by the Patriarch of Jerusalem, Heraclius, who was in England to generate support for the crusaders in the Holy Land. While he was here, he also consecrated the Hospitallers' church of St John (very similar to the Templars'), at their headquarters half a mile to the north, in Clerkenwell.

Above Temple Church suffered catastrophic damage during the Blitz and was not fully repaired for a number of years. The Round Church was rededicated in 1958.
Right Temple Church from the southeast. On the right the steps lead to the Master's House.
Opposite above Temple Church from the south. Eight hundred years of history are shown side by side as the Round Church is partially shadowed by a pillar erected to commemorate the Millennium.

IN SEARCH OF THE KNIGHTS TEMPLAR

The London Temple was one of the three administrative centres of the Order, along with the Paris Temple and their headquarters in Jerusalem. Temple Church was the centre of the Templars' London preceptory, which in turn was the headquarters of the Templar estates in Britain. All their wealth was held here, in a treasury so renowned for security that kings would confidently deposit their own riches there — even their crown jewels. It was here that London's role as a great financial centre began. The original exchequer was probably sited in chambers beneath the church precinct, where a wall was found decorated with the black and white squares used as a visual key to the movement of finances.

Above A plan of the early Temple Church. Note the round nave, a typical architectural style used by the Templars.

Top The only other surviving medieval building is the buttery (a store for food and drink, from the French for 'bottle', *bouteille*) which is situated opposite the church. These are the filled-in archways.

Middle One of the strange 'green men' carved into the arch of the west porch.

Bottom Ornate capitals in the west porch.

Above right The west door, the original main Norman entrance. Around the arch, the Templars carved an assortment of intriguing images.

The Templars, as elsewhere in Europe, became the confidants of kings and nobles; the London Masters were often employed, as was Alan Marcell, in negotiations with foreign powers, or as trusted royal escorts — for example Robert de Sandford, who in 1236 brought Eleanor of Provence to England as the bride of Henry III. The Templars' close relationship with the Crown led to their involvement at key points in history: the murderers of Thomas Becket — secular knights — were ordered to join the Templars in Jerusalem and give land to them as penance; a sword used to kill the archbishop was displayed in the Temple Church. One Master, Brother Aymeric, witnessed the signing of Magna Carta.

Henry III presided over the church's expansion in 1240, when the new chancel was built. He also expressed a wish to be buried there; the church would be his mausoleum — an unorthodox notion. The tomb of a monarch would inevitably be imposing, dominant: contrary to the Templar ethic, which was all to do with plainness and functionality. Knights themselves were usually buried in modest tombs with simple grave slabs — it was their illustrious supporters who were given finely carved effigies. In the event, it seems that Henry changed his will, and he was actually buried in Westminster Abbey.

The Templars did not move entirely in high court circles. Their day-to-day activities would bring them into close contact with the surrounding population — traders, shopkeepers, industrialists, craftsmen, householders of all kinds, as well as members of other monastic houses. One Master of the Temple (at an unspecified date) was embroiled in a matter far removed from affairs of state, when he was summoned in a legal case. A certain Walter Wan of Wendlesworthe had been crossing the Thames near Westminster Bridge when he fell from his boat and drowned. The verdict was misadventure. The law of the time included a principle called 'deodandum' (not abolished until 1846). This stipulated that if a personal possession in motion caused the death of its owner, it should be rendered to God — that is, the Crown—to be employed for pious uses. In this case the boat, valued at ten shillings, was declared deodandum. Apparently the Master of the Temple 'took the boat without warrant' and was directed to make satisfaction for the boat to the Crown, which he duly did.

A more long-running dispute involved the Templars' inconsiderate practice of powering their watermill by damming the River Fleet, which ran down into the Thames (and still does, though now underground). According to Charles Addison, the Templars had caused the river to stagnate, creating a 'great nuisance'. In 1290 the prior of the Carmelites complained that the 'putrid exhalations arising from the Fleet river' were so powerful they overcame the burning of incense and had 'occasioned the deaths of many or their brethren', while other monastic houses within range made similar complaints. Mill owners downstream, deprived of a proper flow of water, added their voices.

Such disputes, as well as every other aspect of the Order's industry and enterprise, would come to an end in December 1307 when the king's men came to the Temple to arrest all the Templars—and found just thirteen, only three of them knights: John de Stoke, the treasurer; Michael de Baskerville, the preceptor; and Ralph de Barton, a priest. These were the three essential officers of a preceptory, true, but curiously few to run the headquarters of the British Order.

Top A number of lost tombs were found in 1861. One revealed an inscription that read 'PHILIPPVS HILARIO', marking the grave of Philip de St Hilaire, a Norman knight. Philip, who died c. 1200, was most likely a Templar. As a younger son, with no substantial inheritance, he was typical of knights in the Holy Land, attracted to the Crusades as a means of acquiring the wealth and land that they would not have at home. **Above** Some of the scattered tombs within the churchyard to the north.

After their arrest, all the Templars endured years of interrogation and imprisonment— though in conditions far less harsh than their French brethren had to suffer. Those who survived incarceration were released in 1311 after pleading guilty to minor charges.

After the official suppression of the Templars in 1312 and by the order of the pope, the Temple, in common with other English properties, was supposed to be handed over to the Hospitallers. In fact the Crown wrangled with them over it, and the Hospitallers did not take possession until 1324. They held the grounds and church before leasing the buildings to the legal profession in around 1347—a connection that persists to this day.

Highlights of the Temple's subsequent history include an attack on it during the Peasants' Revolt. In 1381, after the introduction of the first poll tax, some rebels stormed the Temple, associating it with the hated tax as the king's treasurer at the time was the Master of the Hospitallers, Sir Robert Hales. They eventually found him and hacked off his head, spiking it on Westminster Bridge — but not before they destroyed all the records they found at the Temple. They had earlier sacked another former Templar property, Cressing Temple (see page 87). What knowledge might have been lost can only be guessed at.

By the early 1600s, the church needed extensive—and expensive—repairs. It was lucky to survive the Great Fire of London later that century. On 2 September 1666 buildings in the Temple precincts were blown up in an attempt to arrest the fire's progress westward—fortunately successful. Though the Temple Church was not itself damaged, its interior was modified to some extent by Christopher Wren. Thereafter, the church was repaired and restored at various times. In contrast to today, shops were built close against the church, and not removed until 1819.

The early Victorians gave the church a pointed roof and covered the crenellations around the tower (presumably to protect the building and allow the rain to drain away). During this time the

Above Across the aisle from the south porch half-way up the wall is a window, giving way to a small cell– too small to lie down in. It was in this penitential cell that Walter le Bachelor, the Irish Grand Master, was imprisoned for embezzlement in the early fourteenth century. As a signal of the gravity of his crime, he was left to starve to death in public.

Opposite top Effigies in the centre of the round church. The columns of black Purbeck marble were replaced after the Blitz damage.

Opposite bottom left A gallery of painted grotesque faces adorns the wall above the alcoves.

Opposite bottom right The Templars' round church, superbly restored after being hit by incendiary bombs on the night of 10 May 1941.

IN SEARCH OF THE KNIGHTS TEMPLAR

Above The tomb of
William Marshal, Earl
of Pembroke, in the
foreground. This legendary
knight became a Templar
on his deathbed. Beside
him lies his son and heir,
also called William.
Opposite above Middle
Temple Hall, in the Temple
precincts, is sited on the
same spot as the original
Templars' Great Hall.
Opposite left A grotesque
carving found in the round
nave.
Opposite right A carving
of a knight in chain mail
from the east end of
the chancel.

effigies within the church were moved. They had long ceased to be in their
original positions—some time in the late 1600s, the treasurer of Middle
Temple had carried out the task of 'marshalling the knights Templars in uniform order'. The bodies of the respective knights are likely to be buried
beneath the floor of the church but not under their original tomb lids.

The effigies were badly damaged during the Second World War, when the
church was heavily bombed. They are, however, preserved in their original
form in the 'cast room' of the Victoria and Albert Museum in South Kensing-
ton. These casts were done in the Victorian era when, wisely as it turns out,
enthusiastic antiquarians decided to preserve the past by making exact rep-
licas in plaster, cast from the originals. Here the knights' tomb lids lie, next to
a cast of the 'apprentice pillar' from Rosslyn Chapel (pages 237–9).

The bombing raid and its aftermath were commemorated in a painting by
Kathleen Allen, which now hangs within the south porch.

It took some years for the damage to be rectified. The painstaking restoration work included removing the Victorian 'improvements', and building the

IN SEARCH OF THE KNIGHTS TEMPLAR

present-day main south porch — a chapel to St Anne stood here until it was demolished in 1825. The church was officially rededicated in 1958, and its exterior appearance is now much closer to the original. The interior, however, in common with many other surviving Norman buildings, now lacks the colourful decoration that was common in the Middle Ages.

✝ TO THE NORTH of the church in its paved enclave is the Goldsmith Building (named after the poet Oliver Goldsmith), on what was previously known as Churchyard Court and, for reasons that may be guessed at, Pissing Alley.

The west porch is a thing of beauty in itself, its door arch decorated with images of the 'green man' and other esoteric symbols. There are carvings said to be of American corn, although pine cones have also been suggested.

On the south side of the church is a courtyard with a memorial to the Temple's history. The pillar, showing two knights riding on one horse, was erected for the Millennium; Nicola Hicks sculpted the figures, and Ptolemy Dean designed the pillar and base.

In times past, this area was very crowded, with shops actually leaning against the church. It is from this courtyard that the present-day visitor enters the church, through the south porch.

✠ THE TOWER OF LONDON

The Normans marked their conquest in stone. In London, they built a great fortress on the banks of the Thames, east of the City, and called it the White Tower — the nucleus of what would be the Tower of London. Completed by around 1100, it soon became the principal prison for enemies of the state. It had been standing for just over two centuries when the Templars were suppressed, and it was one of the prisons to which they were brought for interrogation.

As well as the Tower, the Templars were held in the 'gates' of London — fortified buildings such as Aldgate, Ludgate, Newgate, Bishopsgate and Cripplegate. (In Lincoln, prisoners were held in Clasketgate.) The mandate for their arrest, and the audit of their properties, had gone out at the end of 1307, though was not put into effect until the next month. By 1310, those held in the Tower of London were in chains — and may or may not have been facing the prospect of torture.

While torture was a routine part of the French state apparatus, it was not allowed under English law — much to the annoyance of inquisitors who had arrived from France to interrogate the imprisoned Templars. These visitors seemed to feel that interrogation without torture was a waste of time, and even suggested that the prisoners be transferred to France where they would be outside English law and more effective methods of persuasion could be employed.

Eventually the English king, Edward II, allegedly agreed that some 'light' torture could be

Above An atmospheric nineteenth-century engraving of the Tower.
Right A bird's-eye view of the the site. From a survey made in 1597 by order of the Governor of the Tower.

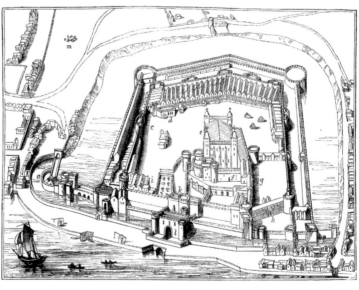

IN SEARCH OF THE KNIGHTS TEMPLAR

applied. Charles Addison is certain that William de la More's declaration of innocence in 1311 (see page 53) enraged his inquisitors, and 'all the engines of terror wielded by the church were put in force', and 'torture was unsparingly applied', the Templars 'suffering under the torments of the rack' as the inquisitors went around the locations in London where the Templars were held in 'loathsome dungeons'.

Some of Addison's sources may have been unreliable — there is no evidence of the rack being used at the time, for example — and the degree to which the Templars were tortured remains unclear. If not physical, though, then psychological torture would have been employed. Prisoners were sometimes introduced to a man called the 'master of torture'. He would just be an officer of the castle, having nothing to do with torture and no doubt chosen for his ominous looks. Many a prisoner, believing the charade, confessed on the spot — as they did when instruments of torture were displayed to them. These methods no doubt added to the stories of actual torture.

Certainly, a few of the brothers died while in captivity, but this may be due to infirmity or the fact that many were already aged.

Above The White Tower at the Tower of London was commissoned by William the Conqueror and completed in 1097.

Whatever the truth of their treatment, eventually most of the English Templars went along with a compromise — they would admit to the fact that the master of a preceptory sometimes gave absolution for sins when in fact he did not have dispensation to do so.

Only William de la More and Himbert Blanke, a visiting French preceptor, refused to admit any irregularities and both died in the Tower. As Addison says, 'a few months after the close of these proceedings brother William de la More the master of the temple in England died of a broken heart in his solitary dungeon in the tower, persisting in his last breath in the maintenance of the innocence of his order'. King Edward then directed the constable of the tower to hand over William's belongings to his executors.

The death of such a renowned knight, the head of a previously mighty order who, most people in England continued to believe, was without blame, has few records — and, after William's death, his body disappeared.

There may be two reasons for this. William might have been allowed a burial at the Temple Church that went unrecorded, as officially he was still outside the Church by continuing to maintain his innocence. Alternatively

—and certainly more speculatively—William's 'death' preserved the king's reputation, and he was allowed to disappear. His continued protestation of innocence from the dungeons of the Tower was a problem for Edward. His 'death' would suit them both.

As ever, where hard fact is elusive, rumours would spread. One of the charges against the Templars, that they worshipped a 'head', had particular resonance for those in the Tower, given that Tower Hill was reputed to be the burial place of Bran the Blessed's severed head (see All Hallows, page 52). According to legend, King Arthur had Bran's head dug up, seeing him as a rival guardian of the land— a story symbolic of Christianity's triumph over paganism.

There is another connection: 'Bran' means 'raven' in Welsh, and the famous ravens of the Tower of London are linked in a mystical way to the wellbeing of the realm. In earlier centuries, the Tower had other animal connections—oddly, in view of its fearsome reputation, in the form of a zoo. The menagerie started in 1235 with a gift of leopards to Henry III, later augmented by the first African elephant in Britain since the Romans and a collection of lions. In the eighteenth century a visitor could feed their pet dog or cat to the lions in lieu of an admission fee. There was also a polar bear that was taken every evening to the Thames on a 'long lead' to catch fish—it escaped and swam upriver, never to be seen again.

Since then, the Tower itself has left its bloody history behind along with its zoo to become the major tourist attraction it is today: a barracks, an armoury, a museum, and the repository of the Crown Jewels.

Above Carvings by prisoners from within the Beauchamp Tower. These are thought to date from the Tudor period.
Right The Norman Chapel, contemporary with the Templars, located within the White Tower.

IN SEARCH OF THE KNIGHTS TEMPLAR

✛ WHERE EXACTLY THE TEMPLARS were imprisoned in the Tower is unknown. Some were said to have been imprisoned in the dungeon called 'little ease'—built into the thickness of a wall, in which the prisoner could neither sit, stand nor lie, but was compelled to serve his sentence in a crouching position. The cell has never been found, though, and there are no official records of its existence.

Much of the Tower seen today was not built in the Templars' time. When they were prisoners the famous White Tower existed, surrounded by the perimeter wall (called a curtain wall), which had towers spaced at regular intervals. These were used to hold prisoners.

The Martin Tower on the northeastern corner was one of these. Today the bottom storey houses the gift shop; inside, to the right of its entrance is carved a Templar cross. Templars elsewhere certainly did carve crosses on the walls of their prisons, but there is no clear evidence as to the author of this carving.

Far more elaborate and extensive graffiti carved by later prisoners can be found in the Beauchamp Tower, sited near the execution block.

Above A Templar cross, carved into stone to the right of the ground-floor entrance to the Martin Tower. This structure was standing at the time of the Templars' arrest and may have been their place of confinement.

THE SOUTHEAST

IN TEMPLAR TIMES, the Southeast of England was similar to how it appears today—in relative terms—in being highly developed and densely populated. The Templars' chief preceptory outside London was at Dinsley, in Hertfordshire; nothing of this now remains, but evidence of the Order still lies scattered in a variety of sites both religious and secular. ✛ Kent had a particular significance, in that the port of Dover was the chief embarkation point for voyages to Europe and the Holy Land—travellers would need guidance and accommodation. The nearest preceptory was at Temple Ewell, where its church of SS Peter and Paul still stands. Many of the knights and pilgrims passing through Temple Ewell would have stayed at Strood Temple Manor on the Medway, now a solitary survivor among a mass of modernity—in its way as lonely as the windswept ruins of the little Templar chapel on the cliffs above Dover. ✛ Three other churches, all dedicated to St Mary, are of special interest. Shipley in West Sussex is a fine example of an early Templar church, while Sompting in Sussex has a unique style of tower, and the church in Selborne, Hampshire, is notable for its Templar grave slabs and beautiful medieval floor. There is another surviving manor house, near Marlow in Buckinghamshire: the well-preserved Bisham Abbey. While not open to the public, its exterior can be appreciated from not far away. In its prime, Bisham would have been part of a preceptory complex that included substantial timber barns for storing grain, similar to the cathedral-like structures that have miraculously survived at Cressing Temple in Essex. ✛ A site unique in the whole country is not a church, or manor house, or farm building — but a cave, lying under an ancient crossroads in the middle of the busy modern town of Royston in Hertfordshire. With its mass of medieval carvings both Christian and pagan, its purpose remains as mysterious as its origins. ✛

✠ SHIPLEY

(WEST SUSSEX) *St Mary's at Shipley is one of the earliest Templar churches in the country, the nave, tower and chancel dating from around 1140 — barely a dozen years after the first visit of Hugh de Payens, the founder of the Templars. But already it signals the characteristics of the Order. A high, spacious building, with a massive central tower and two solid supporting arches, it reflects the growing power and prestige of the Templars, standing as a substantial symbol of enduring faith, while its plain design is appropriate for a monastic order that prizes simplicity and integrity.*

The original manor and land had been bestowed on the Templars in 1139 — one of their earliest endowments — by Philip de Braose. As George Tull notes, Philip made his gift with the words:

> Moved by the words of the gospel, 'give unto Caesar what is Caesar's and unto God what is God's,' and excited by the holy spirit, I give and grant unto God and to the blessed Mary and the soldiers of the temple of Solomon, for ever in perpetual alms a certain portion of the earthly lands which God has granted me to possess in this world namely the land of Herschapelia [Shipley] and the church...

Shipley was a mainly agricultural preceptor — its name comes from the Old English *scēaplēah*, meaning a place where sheep are kept — and even today this pleasant village remains peaceful and unspoilt, and St Mary's continues to function as a parish church.

The church is well known for its Romanesque features, particularly the arch of the west door, and the strange corbels on the first of the massive arches supporting the tower. The beautiful south porch contains a mooring post that is possibly Templar — used perhaps on the River Adur, about a mile away, or on the smaller tributaries that flow through the village.

A few other Templar traces can be seen: evidence of the moat to the north

Previous page A detail of a carving from Royston Cave: two riders on the same horse above a crescent moon.
Right The name Shipley means 'a place where sheep are kept', a tradition maintained to this day.

IN SEARCH OF THE KNIGHTS TEMPLAR

Top left The wooden-framed south porch is thought to be a sixteenth-century addition.

Top right South porch interior. Note the old mooring stone, back right, possibly used by the Templars when they transported men and goods along the local waterways.

Above Detail of Romanesque capital, west porch.

Left The jagged ornamental arch of the west porch suggests it dates from the mid-to-late twelfth century.

Above Ancient paving at the west of the church.
Above right The nineteenth-century windmill stands to the west of the church. The Templars are credited with being the first to introduce the windmill to Europe.
Opposite top Two arches support the massive tower.
Opposite bottom right Detail of floor mosaic near altar.
Opposite middle left Right-hand corbel of the western arch has an equally grotesque twin opposite.
Opposite bottom left Tomb of Sir Thomas Caryll, d. 1617, sited to the south of the altar. It was restored in 1831.

and east of the church, and the preceptory's fishponds to the southeast.

Until quite recently a particularly beautiful Templar artefact could be seen in the church. George Tull describes it:

> A thirteenth-century reliquary which, from its style, was probably made in Limoges. This was in the form of an oakwood casket about seven inches long with a sharply pitched roof, covered in copper and enamelled with Saints and the Crucifixion in gold, dark and light blue; essentially a tiny church or shrine for the Saints whose relics were here. Unfortunately, there is now only a replica of this priceless reliquary to be seen there, as the original was stolen in 1976.

When the Templars were arrested, the audit of their property at Shipley included, as recorded in the Victoria County History, 'a long list of household items and farming implements, a small quantity of armour, twenty silver spoons and a book of kings and a book of beasts'. The manor was valued at £8, the church £13 and the goods £73; this again bears out the values of property when compared to 'goods'—armour and farm tools being particularly valuable.

After the suppression of the Templars, there was the habitual trouble regarding who might use the Order's properties, before the Hospitallers were able to take possession of Shipley, which they held until the Dissolution.

To the west of the church is a much more modern structure, but one that would have been appreciated by the industrious Templars: a windmill. Built in 1879, it was once the home of the writer Hilaire Belloc, and later the fictional home of television sleuth Jonathan Creek.

✠ SOMPTING

(WEST SUSSEX) *Originally Saxon, taken over and expanded by the Templars, St Mary's is probably the oldest and certainly the most unusual of all the churches associated with the Order—indeed, the tower, the oldest part of the church, is now unique in the country, the last remaining example of the so-called 'Rhinish Helm' style. Other Saxon elements have survived in the fabric of the building, including typical high windows and stone pilaster strips. And, just as Saxon meets Norman here, so too do Templars and Hospitallers—each Order having its own surviving chapel.*

The original church had already been in existence for around a century before the Conquest. In 1154 it was granted to the Templars, who soon rebuilt the nave and chancel on the original Saxon plan. They also added the present north and south transepts, both of which were separated from the main church, functioning as small private chapels for the use of the Order.

The south transept, built in 1180, is lower than the rest of the church and has its own small chancel and sacristy. On its west window is the arch of an original Norman window, and on the east wall a carving of an abbot. The south door on to this chapel was originally much higher, possibly to admit men holding banners. The Norman font stands on a modern pillar, to the right of which is a piscina.

At the base of the tower, which incorporates some old Roman stones, is a Saxon arch, with carved capitals. This arch is not placed centrally and may have accommodated an altar. The carved capitals are foliate, in common with the Ringerike, or early Viking, style.

Attached to the north side of the tower is a small flint Hospitaller chapel, which stood for some time as a ruin before being repaired and reroofed—today it continues in its original role, as a chapel for the St John Ambulance.

✛ WESTERN HEIGHTS

(DOVER, KENT) The simplest of Templar sites: the ruins of a small flint chapel standing on high ground to the west of the town, on the appropriately named Western Heights—just a round nave, so small that it needed no supporting pillars, and a rectangular chancel. In its time it would have stood alone on the top of the cliff, with whitewashed walls and perhaps a timber or thatched roof, a place of worship for Templars embarking for the Holy Land, and a conspicuous landmark to welcome them home. Unlike many Templar properties, it was never rebuilt or expanded.

The Templar round church at another port, Bristol, had almost exactly the same dimensions as the one at Dover: the circular nave 32 feet in diameter; the chancel 26 feet long and 20 feet wide. And it would have been used in very much the same way, by knights preparing to leave for the Holy Land, or—if they survived the multitude of hazards—returning home.

Nothing specific is known about the modest Dover chapel under the Templars, though it might have been the site of King John's humiliating submission to the papal legate that ended his dispute with the pope. In due course, and unlike Bristol and other round churches, it was left to fall into disuse and ruin, though the preceptory to which it was attached, Temple Ewell, reflected the Templars' prosperity and expanded dramatically (see page 82).

Given its elevated position, the Dover chapel could well have doubled as a lookout point in troubled times; later threats to national security led to its rediscovery. When the great defence works were being built on the Western Heights in the early nineteenth century against the expected French invasion under Napoleon, the remains of the little chapel were uncovered.

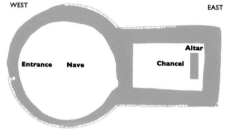

WEST   EAST

Altar

Entrance   Nave   Chancel

Above A plan of the round church at Dover.
Right Looking over the port of Dover from Western Heights, the site of the Templars' church.
Opposite top The remains of the small medieval flint church.
Opposite bottom left Church from the southwest.
Opposite bottom right Detail of the doorway into the western end of the church.

     IN SEARCH OF THE KNIGHTS TEMPLAR

✛ STROOD TEMPLE MANOR

(KENT) *The manor house is all that remains of the preceptory on the banks of the Medway, surrounded by modern industrial developments. It once saw a very different kind of activity — on the direct route from London to Dover, it would accommodate travellers going to and from the Holy Land and other places of pilgrimage. With the Templars' international web of transport and business links, the manor may well have functioned rather like a modern hotel, taking bookings as part of a package tour.*

The original estate pre-dated the manor house by some years. A gift of King Henry II, Strood was up and running by the inquest (inventory) of 1185, indicating that it had been founded some years before — George Tull suggests a date of 1159 at the latest. It was a large estate, including a timber hall, kitchens, stables and barns. The manor was built in 1240; it would be enclosed with extensions at either end in the seventeenth century, and would be inhabited one way or another until the twentieth.

The river of course was an important highway, though today a modern building obscures its proximity to the manor. In the Templars' time it would have flowed just to the east, an area still called Temple Marsh (and Strood itself gets its name from the Old English for 'marsh', *strôd*). On the opposite bank stands Rochester Castle. Strood's other vital transport link was the old Roman road of Casing Street, running close to the manor and up to London near to the Order's headquarters, and joining with Watling Street that continues on to Shropshire.

At the western end of Casing Street was Dover, an embarkation point for the long journey to the Holy Land for pilgrims and crusaders. A small Templar round chapel was built on the hills overlooking Dover as a place where prayers could be said for a safe journey or thanks for a safe return (see

Right Strood Manor. The central stone section is Templar, sandwiched by the later redbrick sections. **Opposite** The undercroft, probably used for storage, with the main living area directly above.

page 76). Pilgrims could have also been headed for Santiago de Compostela in Spain, as evidenced by the number of churches dedicated to St James along the way (Santiago being the Spanish for St James).

With their international connections, the Templars were able to facilitate such journeys. Travellers could plan their route and book at one of the preceptories, depositing money with the Order to be withdrawn in Europe or the Middle East. They could stop along the way in Templar residences and voyage in ships owned or leased by the Templars.

There were obvious advantages for the traveller in such an arrangement. He would not be vulnerable to being robbed or getting lost, and he would have continual care and advice—the Templars seeing to his material concerns while he was able to concentrate on his pilgrimage.

Strood Manor was also well placed to accommodate pilgrims to the most popular English shrine in the thirteenth century: that of Thomas Becket at Canterbury. Becket had been made a saint in 1173, three years after his murder. As a penance, his murderers were directed to join the Templars for fourteen

Above South wall of
the Templars' building.
Above right Detail of the
external western wall of the
Templars' building, visible
internally on the top floor of
a later western extension.
Above middle right
A seventeenth-century
fireplace in the middle floor
of the western extension.
Right The Templars'
original floor, with
later fireplace.
**Opposite bottom
right** Strood Manor
from the north.
Opposite bottom left
Entrance to the first floor.
The entrance to the
undercroft is directly below.

IN SEARCH OF THE KNIGHTS TEMPLAR

years; they died in the Holy Land where the tombs of two of them remain outside the al-Aqsa mosque.

In 1314, after the suppression of the Templars, all their lands throughout Christendom were granted by the Pope to the Knights Hospitaller, and Strood Manor should have been included—but, as was often the case elsewhere, the Crown was unwilling to give up property it had taken in the intervening period, from the arrests in 1307. In fact Strood was never possessed by the Hospitallers, who eventually gave up trying and ceded it to the king in 1324. Little is known of the tenants, but it seems likely that from this point it functioned as a farm and continued as such up until the twentieth century.

The estate was gradually sold off until what was left was acquired by the city of Rochester in the 1930s. The manor survived the war, but by then was a ruin damaged further by fire and vandals. It was not until 1951 that any work was started to preserve it; over the years it was restored to its present state. Rather like Denny Abbey (page 128), Strood Manor has become an architectural jigsaw that reflects its history.

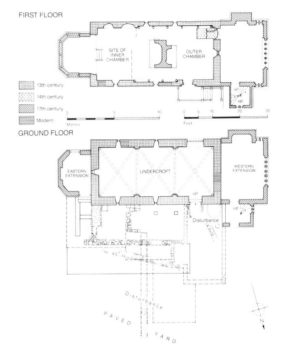

FIRST FLOOR

13th century
14th century
17th century
Modern

GROUND FLOOR

✝ FACING THE NORTH WALL of the manor from the road, three separate areas are visible: the undercroft, the thirteenth-century hall and the seventeenth-century addition to the right. The Templar sections are the undercroft and the hall directly above.

✛ TEMPLE EWELL

(KENT) *The Templars built the Church of SS Peter and Paul, replacing a wooden Saxon church, when they founded the preceptory at Ewell some time before 1164 — in the early years of the Order's existence. It would have initially been a fairly modest establishment, serving as a stopping point for Templars on their way to and from the port of Dover a few miles away — the main embarkation point to the Holy Land and pilgrimage sites in Europe. In time, the human traffic increased as much as the volume of trade, and Temple Ewell became a significant centre, the Templar Order as a whole becoming the first major multinational corporation.*

Below Tokens of the Templar heritage of Ewell. The sign is from the Templar Pilgrimage Trust giving notice of the adoption of the church as the 'guild church' for the trust.
Opposite top The Church of St Peter and St Paul from the southeast.
Opposite bottom The church from the southwest.

While the church has survived through the centuries, nothing remains of the preceptory. There is a link with King John, though: a close associate of the Order who was known to stay at Ewell.

One particularly humiliating occasion in John's career brought him to Ewell, a couple of years before he was to accede to Magna Carta. He had been disputing with the Pope about who had the right to appoint the Archbishop of Canterbury — the Pope and his representatives, or the king. The Pope proclaimed an interdict against England in 1207, effectively leaving the population without the comforts of the Church and the lifeline to Rome. John retaliated by seizing Church property and behaving in a provocative manner. In 1209 he himself was excommunicated, and in 1213 he was told to submit to the Vatican or face the consequences.

John knew he was in an awkward position as without the support of the Church he was open to attack from ambitious barons. There was no alternative, and the king made his submission to the papal legate, Pandulph, on 15 May 1213.

Where the actual event took place is unclear. Matthew Paris, the historian monk of St Albans, states that King John met the legate 'in the house of the

IN SEARCH OF THE KNIGHTS TEMPLAR

Templars near Dover'—but whether this was at Ewell or the Templars' small round church on the cliffs above the port (see page 76) is not known. He certainly did stay at Ewell preceptory, though.

After the suppression of the Templars in 1314, the Knights Hospitaller took over the manor at Temple Ewell.

That the preceptory had had a modest beginning, and developed as its importance grew, was borne out by a survey of the site by the Reverend Hales in 1864. He found the remains of several buildings and a tiny chapel, 15 feet by 15 feet. He also found evidence that the buildings had been enlarged and extensions built.

IN SEARCH OF THE KNIGHTS TEMPLAR

Left A tomb lid, said to be of Templar origin.
Opposite top A Templar cross, one of a few carved in stone, on the left side of the north entrance.
Opposite bottom left The church interior looking west. The church is set into a hill so the western entrance is higher than the floor of the nave, necessitating eight stone steps.

Above A medieval carving found on a Romanesque capital located by the north entrance.
Opposite bottom right A seventeenth-century Swiss stained-glass window, a feature of this church found in the north wall. There are many different scenes; this is Mary, Joseph [carrying his saw] and the infant Jesus.

✛ CRESSING TEMPLE

(ESSEX) *Other Templar preceptories have left their monuments in stone, with remains of church or manor house or outbuilding. Cressing is unique in that what has endured here was made of wood—the very material least likely to survive the rigours of climate and the danger of fire. Through a mixture of luck and excellent building techniques, two huge timber-framed barns are still standing, magnificent structures with the internal space and proportions of a cathedral. Designed to hold grain, they are monuments to the enormous wealth accumulated by the Templars through agriculture and trade.*

Cressing was the first recorded Templar property outside London, donated by Queen Matilda, the wife of King Stephen; the Order later gained the nearby land of Witham through Stephen's donation.

It is perhaps ironic that the Templars established themselves and expanded during one of the most destructive periods in English history: the civil wars between Stephen and his cousin the Empress Matilda—appropriately known as the anarchy, from 1135 to 1154. Matilda (also called Maud, and not to be confused with Stephen's wife) was the daughter of Henry I and effectively first in line to the throne; however, on Henry's death, Stephen had himself proclaimed king.

England was then plunged into chaos, nobles choosing allegiance to either Stephen or Matilda. King David of Scotland supported Matilda, but was defeated at the Battle of Northallerton. Stephen was then defeated at the Battle of Lincoln, where he was captured along with other nobles (including the prominent Templar supporter Roger de Mowbray—see page 184). The following year Stephen was released and the civil war started up again, until both parties eventually came to an understanding. Matilda left England in 1147, and the enfeebled Stephen was allowed to remain nominally on the throne until his death, when he would be succeeded by Matilda's son, as Henry II.

Opposite top The barley barn. Constructed in the Romanesque tradition of carpentry of the early thirteenth century, it was built of 480 oak trees felled between 1205 and 1235.
Opposite middle Two views of the wheat barn, which was built fifty years after its neighbour.
Below The moat at Cressing Temple.

The war between Stephen and Matilda has a bearing on the Templars in that the Order received property from both parties. These donations probably had dual motives: gaining the political support of the Templars, as well as having them pray for the souls of the benefactors. Certainly the knights could not have taken part in the conflict themselves, being forbidden to fight fellow Christians.

Queen Matilda, Stephen's wife, also had a crusading connection in that she was a niece of Baldwin, the first king of Jerusalem. Certainly her donation would have been highly appreciated by the Templars—it was a propitious site, with fertile soil and good transport links by both road and river. Cressing Temple expanded gradually as the Order received small donations, and by the end of the twelfth century had about 160 tenants. The Templars

established a market here to capture all the potential customers who were travelling between London and the then major town of Colchester.

The inventory taken after the suppression details the buildings extant at that time: a chapel, two chambers, a hall, pantry, buttery (a room for storing food or drink), kitchen, larder, bakehouse, brewery, dairy, granary and smithy, with stock including horses, cattle, pigs, sheep, geese, hens and peacocks. The two great wooden barns are called the wheat barn and the barley barn.

With the end of the Order, Cressing joined the rest of the Templar possessions in being handed over to the Hospitallers. One of their later masters, Sir Robert Hales, was to have a violent end. During the Peasants' Revolt of 1381, Sir Robert was also the Treasurer of England and responsible for the hated poll tax, the spark that lit the fire of the revolt. The rebels started by sacking his manor at Cressing, but he was in London at the time. When Wat Tyler and his men caught up with him taking refuge in the Tower of London, they beheaded him (see page 60).

During this revolt much of the Templars' records at Cressing and London were lost, the peasants burning everything they found. What was lost of Templar history during this indiscriminate destruction will never be known.

Above The seal of Walter Fitzstephens, a Templar scribe, found during recent excavations.

Above The wheat barn interior, demonstrating the intricate but robust carpentry that created this wooden cathedral.
Below left The Cressing Temple complex from the south.
Below right A Templar initiation scene has been re-created in the wheat barn. Here, a guard bars the entrance.
Opposite above A detail of the structure of the Barley barn drawn by David Stenning.
Opposite below The barley barn.

✠ THE SITE IS A MIXTURE of buildings from all ages, the earliest being Templar: the two barns, and also a well that has recently been uncovered to view. The well, skilfully made of ashlar masonry, is about 45 feet deep. Just above the water line is a bricked-up arch, an entrance — but to where? The theories range from legends of Templars' tunnels to a prosaic drain.

Approaching the barns from the main entrance, the wheat barn stands to the right, the barley barn to the left. In the wheat barn a new steel walkway provides the opportunity to view the beams up close. There is also a permanent exhibition here, featuring models in medieval dress, including a Templar knight standing guard over an initiation ceremony.

The foundations of the chapel have been identified just to the south of the garden, although nothing is visible today. As with many other Templar chapels and churches, it is aligned a few degrees to the north of east. The reason for this is not altogether clear, but may reflect the position of the sun rising on the particular feast day of the dedicated patron saint. At Cressing, a market was held on the feast day of St John the Baptist. On this day the sun would rise a few degrees to the north of east. (See Appendix.)

IN SEARCH OF THE KNIGHTS TEMPLAR

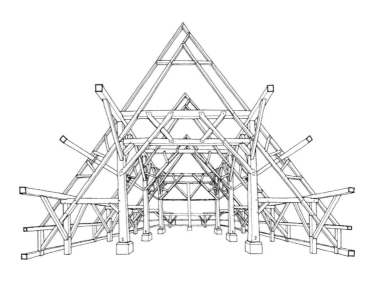

✛ BISHAM ABBEY

(BERKSHIRE) This is not an abbey but a manor house, part of a preceptory built by the Templars on the banks of the Thames — strategically sited to take advantage of the river route between Templar properties in London and Sandford in Oxfordshire. The preceptory at Bisham was spread out, and other buildings were sited where the village of Temple now stands about a mile along the Thames to the north of the abbey, next to Temple Farm, and down Temple Lane — here, as elsewhere, memories of the Order linger in placenames, centuries after the knights themselves have left.

Despite its name, the abbey was never used by a monastic order. In 1337, a priory for Austin canons was founded in the grounds, independent of the house, but nothing of this building remains.

The original land and manor were granted to the Templars by Robert de Ferrers, Earl of Derby, in the reign of King Stephen (1135–54). The house was to have a long and chequered history — at one point acquiring its own ghost — before becoming what it is today, the home of the National Sports Council. As such, it is not open to the public, though occasionally tours are organised by local historical groups. The exterior can easily be viewed across the river from the scenic Thames path that leads east from the village.

Of what remains today, the Templars built the porch, hall, solar (the upper chamber of a medieval house), undercroft and offices.

At the trial of the Templars, Bisham was cited by a witness in relation to accusations of idol worship. John de Donyngton, an ex-Templar and now a member of the Minorites, another monastic order, said he had heard that the Templars were in possession of four 'heads': one in London, one at Temple Bruer, one at Bisham and a fourth at a place north of the Humber. These heads were rumoured to have magical properties (see Templecombe, page 110).

Below Bisham Abbey is a mixture of building styles and materials, most of the stone sections are likely to be Templar with red brickwork added later.

After the suppression, the Hospitallers apparently took possession in 1320, but had difficulty retaining the property when Edward II gave it to his lover Hugh Despenser, who was later beheaded. However, E.T. Lang states that, along with the Temple in London, the Hospitallers were excluded by the king from taking possession of Bisham—although that may be incorrect as the Temple in London actually was passed on to the Hospitallers.

On the first floor of the manor, there is a room dedicated to Henry VIII— he stayed here to escape the plague in London. Henry handed over Bisham as part of his divorce settlement with Anne of Cleves, but she was asked to move to a similar house by Edward VI, who gave Bisham to Sir Philip Hoby in 1552.

Both Henry and Elizabeth I held council meetings at Bisham. It would have been familiar to the queen, who had spent some time here as a guest of the Hobys, under 'house arrest' by her sister Mary Tudor.

The owners and residents of Bisham appear to have experienced a catalogue of misfortune. Many of the Hoby family maintained ambivalent relations with the Crown and a good number of the men and one woman

Top Bisham Abbey from the south. In *Three Men in a Boat* Jerome K. Jerome notes that Bisham Abbey 'contains a tapestry bed-chamber, and a secret room hid high up in the thick walls'.
Above left Bisham Abbey from the southeast, showing the bay window of the 'Elizabeth Room' – Elizabeth I held council meetings here.
Above right Looking out from the undercroft of the abbey, to the tennis courts and training centre of the National Sports Council.

ended up on the block. The ghost of Margaret Hoby is said to have been seen on many occasions in one of the upper rooms, constantly washing her hands in shame — trying to atone for the death of her son whom she beat to death for literally blotting his copy book (the writing book used by a child in the age of inkwells and quills). Eerily, in 1860 a child's notebook of the period was found in the house, full of blots.

At the northeastern end of the great hall, a filled-in window has wall paintings, both modern and some restored from an original painting of SS Peter and John the Evangelist. John was the disciple who underwent a trial by drinking a cup of snake's venom. He survived this, and the snake and chalice became his symbol.

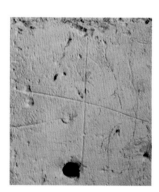

✠ SELBORNE

(HAMPSHIRE) *There was a church on this site before the Conquest; the Normans rebuilt St Mary's, in the form it is today. Nearby was the Templar preceptory of Temple Sotherington, of which nothing remains, and little is known. The main source of information is Selborne's most celebrated resident, the naturalist Gilbert White (1720–93), who is commemorated in the church. White's Natural History and Antiquities of Selborne (1789) became an international bestseller, acutely documenting his observations of flora and fauna around his village—and, more pertinent to the Templars, its history. Being curate of St Mary's, he had access to the medieval records relating to the Order's presence here.*

According to White, the Order once had 'considerable property' in the area, but by his time all that remained of the nearby preceptory was 'a common farm house', with a chapel 'whose massive thick walls, and narrow windows at once bespeak great antiquity ... it has at present much more the appearance of a dungeon than of a room fit for the reception of people of condition.' Today the church contains tomb lids described as 'Templar'; there is also an ornate tiled floor, again possibly Templar.

Above The beautifully detailed tiled floor in the south aisle.

Left Looking east towards the altar, note the solid Norman pillars.

Opposite top left St Mary's from the south.

Opposite bottom left In common with many Templar churches, the figure of John the Baptist is represented. Here, in his usual ragged clothes, he carries his symbol, the lamb and flag.

Opposite right One of three Templar tomb lids to be seen in the church.

✠ ROYSTON CAVE

(HERTFORDSHIRE) *Hollowed out in the distant past by unknown hands, its chalk face would be adorned with fantastic medieval carvings, only to be covered and lost for four hundred years until pure chance again revealed its presence. Royston Cave is unique—the embodiment of the legendary Templar obsession with subterranean chambers and mysterious hidden passages, buried below an Iron Age track where it crosses with a Roman road. Its walls are a riot of images both Christian and pagan, both familiar and, finally, inscrutable. It remains one of the most mysterious sites in the country.*

Stories of Templars building tunnels have largely been attributed to local medieval superstition, which seizes on the nefarious reputation of the knights and in a Freudian-like shift creates myths about the demonic Order and their secret underground activities. Of course, the most obvious explanation is that they really did build many underground spaces, for whatever reason: a covert escape route, a private chapel, hidden storage for supplies ... They lived in a tumultuous age and, at the very least, the pragmatic Templars would build for contingencies.

The discovery in 1994 of a large Templar tunnel running under the port of Acre, which seems to have been built for purely strategic reasons, would appear to support the practical unromantic thesis. It also gives rise to the intriguing thought that maybe there are still many Templar tunnels and caverns to be found under the fields and moors where legend suggests they exist.

Royston Cave, though, while evidently serving certain of the Templars' needs, does not lend itself so readily to a straightforward explanation. Some would see significance in its very location: the cave is beneath the crossroads of two of the most ancient roads in England; Ermine Street (here King Street follows the route), built by the Romans but following older tracks, and the prehistoric Icknield Way (here Melbourn Street).

Right The entrance to Royston Cave is through the door to the left of the bookshop. The cave is actually sited beneath the manhole in the foreground. **Opposite** A depiction of the Crucifixion, one of several to be found in Royston Cave.

It must be said that the Templars' link to the cave remains largely circumstantial, but is now widely accepted. The Order held a market here. The carvings are symbolically consistent with other known Templar work and represent saints favoured by the Order. It is indisputable that the knights were in the local area—they founded the nearby town of Baldock, its name providing a link with the Order's reason for existence. The knights originally called it Baldac, the Old French word for Baghdad, a beguiling echo of their work in the East.

IN SEARCH OF THE KNIGHTS TEMPLAR

Local researcher and historian Sylvia Beamon has conducted exhaustive investigations into the cave, and in her wide-ranging book *Royston Cave: Used by Saints or Sinners?* she confirms the connection with the Templars.

Whatever the Templars' association with the cave, at one point its presence was obliterated and forgotten for centuries—until 1742, by which time a dairy market was held in Royston above the very spot. The market women wanted a new bench and, in putting down a post, workmen discovered a millstone just beneath the surface. Once they had removed this, they could see a shaft disappearing down into the chalk. A small boy was the first 'volunteer' to explore the shaft, and he reported that it went down some way; a 'slender man with a candle' was then found and he reported that the shaft opened up into a chamber filled with loose earth.

This immediately suggested 'buried treasure'. There was a local legend that the founder of Royston, Lady Roisia de Vere (after whom the town was named), had hidden a hoard of valuables somewhere—and the people proceeded to empty the chamber of its contents. And out with the earth went any clues that modern archaeologists would have investigated.

After working continuously through the night and removing 'two hundred loads of earth' the workers were quite exhausted, but had found no treasure. Just 'some small bones, shards of pottery, a human skull and a piece of unmarked brass'; later a seal with a fleur-de-lis design was handed in.

Above Lady Roisia's stone, sited today at the crossroads just up from the cave. There was originally a pillar or post of some sort fixed into the hole.
Right Looking up from the cave to the manhole portrayed on page 96. Originally the cave had an upper floor, where more carvings are visible. The two recesses are old passageways into the cave.

IN SEARCH OF THE KNIGHTS TEMPLAR

What was revealed, though, was a cavern, the walls of which were covered with medieval carvings that had been hidden for centuries.

The antiquarian William Stukeley wrote shortly after the discovery:

> this agreeable subterranean recess, hewn out of pure chalk. 'Tis of an elegant bell like form ... all around the sides, it is adorned with imagery in basso relieve of crucifixes, saints, martyrs and historical pieces ... suitable to a time that was soon after the conquest.

In 1790 a local builder took it upon himself to facilitate a more convenient access to the cave than the rope ladder that had so far been used. No doubt he was motivated by profit, since the new passage he cut started from his own house and he was able to make a small charge for a tour. This is the passage in use today.

Recently there has been more evidence of subterranean features in the area. Details of Templar tunnels in Hertford have come to light, and Sylvia Beamon has reported the existence of a further cavern in Royston: 'There is another cavity in Royston, picked up by underground radar, which I have tried to get investigated to no avail. It is supposed to be 11 feet wide and 18 feet deep and lies in the road close to the pedestrian lights near the church.'

Above The entrance to Royston Cave. The floor plan of the cave was originally octagonal, this has strong links with other Templar octagonal structures such as the round churches.

The known cave has naturally prompted all manner of theories about its origin and function. Stukeley's theory was that the cave was connected with Lady Roisia, and that the carvings were scenes associated with her life. This is now known to be incorrect — even her existence is in doubt. Other theories followed, a popular one in the age of gothic literature being that it was the home of a hermit.

In 1884 Joseph Beldam published *The Origins and Use of the Royston Cave*, which made the first link with the crusaders. He suggests that the cave was ancient, but then converted for Christian purposes by knights as part of their tradition in re-creating buildings they had come across in the Holy Land: 'no greater act of piety could then be imagined than the founding and endowing oratories and hermitages, resembling those that had been devoutly visited and venerated in the Holy Land'.

Beldam then goes on to identify possible crusading families in the area that might be given credit for the cave. What is interesting in Beldam's book is the fact that he never mentions the Templars, just 'Christian knights,'

Below left Stukeley's 1742 drawing of some of the cave figures.

Bottom left Sylvia Beamon suggests this carving is of St George. There is also the possibility of it being Christ and his disciples, as the sword is linked at the top to thirteen figures.

Below right This sun symbol may balance against the moon symbol found elsewhere in the cave.

Bottom right King David is represented up to his waist in water, an image taken literally from the psalm 'Save me O God, for the waters are come into my soul'.

demonstrating that even as recently as 1884 their influence on local early-medieval life had not been fully recognised.

Also absent from pre-modern reports is the mention of the 'sheela na gig' represented among the carvings. This is a female figure depicted with enlarged sexual organs that she is often manipulating to display to best effect. She may be a warning to women of rampant sexuality, or a celebration of fertility and the feminine that was prevalent among the Celts and Anglo-Saxons. Her popularity in the UK and Ireland suggests that she certainly had relevance, whatever her message — a message that evidently had to be toned down in the interests of propriety. In Stukeley's 1742 drawing of the figure, the sheela has acquired a skirt.

The images as a whole here have some similarities with other known Templar carvings at the castles of Chinon and Lincoln.

✝ THE FOLLOWING IMAGES start from the left of the cave's entrance. The descriptions are drawn from Sylvia Beamon's extensive research.

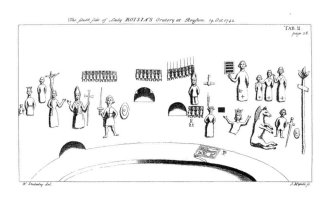

Left The floriated cross also occurs in carvings at Domme in France attributed to the Templars.
Below Images usually thought to represent Mary, Joseph and the infant Jesus, marked by crosses.
Bottom right One of the most significant icons in the cave: a hand with a heart, and a double axe. Similar to symbols carved by the Order at Chinon Castle.
Bottom left The archaeologist T.C. Lethbridge thought this group represented the pagan deities.

Above left The Templar churches in Cornwall and Bristol are dedicated to St Catherine. She is seen here crowned with a fleur-de-lis incorporated into the crown. The Battle of Ramleh on 25 November 1177, in which Templars were involved, occurred on St Catherine's Day and ended in victory. She was little known in the West prior to the crusades.

Above right This lesser Crucifixion scene takes the same form as the main depiction.

Right This main Crucifixion scene is consistent with twelfth-century imagery. Below the arms of the cross are two hands with a heart on the palm of each.

Above This row of figures is thought to be local nobles, or possibly Templars.

Far left The left-hand figure with a crown hovering above her head is thought to be Berengaria, queen of King Richard I. The hovering crown is a symbol of her never having set foot in England.

Left This is rendered in the style of medieval wall paintings. Stukeley noted that St Christopher was used as a form of protection against tempests and earthquakes, and his cult was imported from the Holy Land.

THE SOUTHWEST

ROM THE FLOURISHING PORT of Bristol to a remote outpost on Bodmin Moor, the Templars' presence in the Southwest of England took various forms. One defining factor was the infrastructure for the overland transport of the time, the old Roman roads, which stopped at Exeter. Beyond, there was a mixture of moor and lowland, the tors of Dartmoor and Bodmin Moor, treacherous land that needed a sure guide — packhorse country rather than wagons. ✠ On Bodmin Moor the Templars established the preceptory of Temple. They may also have had a house at Trebeigh, to the south, but this is unclear. Trebeigh may have belonged to the Hospitallers, who then took over Temple on the suppression of the Order. ✠ In sharp contrast to rural isolation, Bristol was well served by the old roads and had grown into a major city and port. Here, as elsewhere in Britain, the Templars marked out their properties by fixing an iron cross to an outside wall. This indicated that the house and its occupants enjoyed a kind of 'tax free' status from the Crown — any taxes or rents the Templars collected went to them. This practice often led to disputes, less fortunate householders accusing the Templars of favouritism when choosing their tenants. ✠ Other western properties were Temple Rockley, near Marlborough; Temple Guiting, between Cheltenham and Banbury; and Templecombe in Somerset. These preceptories were sited in fertile countryside with the option for sheep or pig farming. Apart from the fields, which often continue to follow the boundaries set by the Templars, little remains of their presence except in Templecombe, where the church of St Mary has an intriguing Templar panel painting. ✠

✝ TEMPLE CHURCH

(BRISTOL) *The church today is just a shell, a ruin — yet it still retains much of its historical character, evoking its original purpose as the place of worship for Templars preparing to take ship for the Holy Land, or returning home. At this time, Bristol was a major port, second only to London in importance, and a busy hub of trade and commerce as well as the embarkation point for crusaders and pilgrims. It was another conflict, centuries later, that was to devastate the church — but leave a singular part of it standing.*

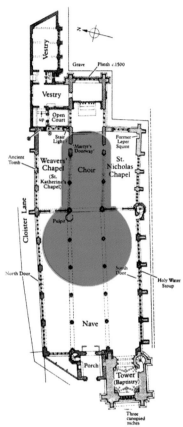

This church is not the first built by the Templars on the site. The first, dedicated to the Holy Cross, was built around 1140 when the Order was given some land known as Temple Fee (which much later became Temple Meads). This was to become the artisans' and craftsmen's quarter of the city. The Templars built their house and a small oval church measuring 50 feet by 30 feet, on practically the same plan as Dover.

By 1299, it is known that a chapel, named for St Katherine, was in use. This was probably an addition to the small chancel of the old 'round' church, and would have been sited on the northern side. It was used by members of the Weavers' Guild — an important group in an area grown rich on the wool trade — and so was known as the Weavers' Chapel. This chapel is the oldest part of the current church, which was built over the foundations of the first at around this time — a fact forgotten by history until 1840, when repair work exposed those original foundations.

Whether the old or the new church was ever part of an actual preceptory is unclear. George Tull states: 'Strangely, it seems Bristol was not a preceptory despite its importance.' He suggests it was run from Templecombe or Temple Guiting, and that the preceptory of Templecombe was founded by Templars from Bristol. Evelyn Lord, however, gives Bristol the status of full preceptory: 'From the Bristol preceptory the Templars administered an inland estate that ran as far as Cornwall.'

Whatever its specific status, Bristol was along with London a major Templar centre and port. The Order was able to expand its operations in Bristol, again like London leaving evidence in street names: Temple Road, Temple Back, Temple Bridge, Temple Court, Temple Gate, Temple Inn Lane, Temple Rose Street, Temple Street, Temple Way and many others.

During the time of the Crusades, embarking for the Holy Land must have been a stirring occasion, a bustling, colourful confusion of men, horses, equipment and provisions, the local population cheering the crusaders on. George Tull quotes from an account by the monk Matthew Paris as the Templars left for their duty overseas:

Previous page Cornish wheel-headed cross, Bodmin Moor.
Above The outline of the original round church, superimposed over the later structure.
Opposite top Corbel on the exterior piscina, eastern end of the church.
Opposite bottom The leaning tower from the southeast.

They set out passing through the town with spears held aloft, shields displayed and piebald banners advanced in unbroken formation and sought a blessing from the people who crowded to see them pass. The brethren uncovered, bowed their heads from side to side, and recommended themselves to the prayers of all.

Tull points out that the quote is particularly significant in that it shows the Templars as being popular with the locals, during a period they were said to be haughty and despised.

For all the fanfare of their send-off, by the time of the Third Crusade—proclaimed by Pope Gregory VIII on 29 October 1187—the crusaders would have been all too aware of the reality of the expedition. The death rate of the first two Crusades had seen a mere fraction of the army return home. Most of the crusaders knew they were saying goodbye to their homeland for good. Some would choose to stay in the Holy Land and carve out a life there. But most would be giving their lives to serve Jesus Christ.

Templar ships would move out into the Bristol Channel, and past Lundy Island, which was apparently given to the Order in the reign of Henry II (1154–89). Whether any Templar ever set foot on the island is unclear, though it has a so-called

'Knights Templar Rock' jutting out into the channel. The next port of call would be La Rochelle, the Templar port in France. From here, there was the choice of going overland through the Templar countryside of the Languedoc, and sailing from Marseilles, or taking a dangerous sea route through the straits of Gibraltar, which were controlled by Islamic forces.

When the time of the Templars had run out, and the Bristol church had new owners, it was given a main tower, which to this day leans at a dramatic angle. This lean was noticed in 1390 when the tower was half-built, and work was stopped. In 1460, once it was decided that the tower would not lean any further, the building work was finished. An attempt was made to build the top vertical, but there was then some more subsidence. Local legend claims the tower leans because the foundations were made from woolsacks—a link to the Weavers' Chapel, perhaps—though the prosaic reason is the underlying marshy land.

The church, complete with leaning tower, continued in service for centuries. *Matthews' Directory* of 1793 describes it:

> This Church seems to have been built at different times, is spacious and lofty, and after Redcliff Church the largest in Bristol. There is an elegant gilded organ on a gallery over the western door; and the long aisles, large windows and arches, lofty ceiling, slender pillars and light open area, have a pleasing effect on spectators. The altar is rich, and adorned with four fine paintings ... It has 3 aisles, and is from East to West 159 feet, and 59 wide, the middle aisle is 50 feet high.

Having painted such a delightful picture, attention now turns to the church's odd appendage:

> But one of the greatest curiosities of Bristol, is the leaning tower of Temple, the foundation of which has so sunk, that it is widely separated from the wall of the Church, and so impends at the southwest corner as to appear ready to tumble down. It is a venerable monument of antiquity; and though so lofty as 112 feet (ending in a plain cornice, without rail, battlement or pinnacle) contains a good peal of 8 bells ... it is said that when these are rung in full peal, if a basin full of water be put on the leads of the tower, it will soon be emptied by the vibration of this apparently precarious yet permanent structure.

The tower has indeed proved to be 'permanent', even surviving the German bombing raid in the Second World War that reduced the church to a ruin. It had a narrow escape, though—from the British army. Sappers sent to make the building safe thought the tower had been knocked sideways by the bomb blast and decided to blow it up. They were informed just in time that the tower had in fact been leaning for five centuries and could safely be left well alone.

Above The tower leans westward not because of Second World War bomb damage, but because it was originally built on marshy ground.
Opposite top Looking from the east over the ruins.
Opposite bottom The grand entrance to Temple Church and park.

IN SEARCH OF THE KNIGHTS TEMPLAR

✝ THE RUINOUS STATE of the church makes it unsafe to enter, and it is not open to the public except on rare occasions. Fortunately, much of the internal structure can be viewed from the outside.

The church precinct is entered from the west gate. A mixture of features can be seen on the external wall such as carved heads over a recess in the east wall and a water stoup on the south. To the left of the west gate there are also some steps that belong to a modern building—climbing these does give a better view of the floor of the church, where the outline of the ancient Templar round church has been delineated by stone markers.

✠ TEMPLECOMBE

(SOMERSET) *Fifty years ago, a hidden treasure was discovered completely by chance in the village of Templecombe. Molly Drew, the tenant of a cottage in West Court, just off the High Street, was in the outhouse collecting wood when she happened to look up at the ceiling. A piece of plaster had fallen down, dislodged by a recent storm, and the painted face of a man was looking back down at her — a face that had not seen the light for at least six hundred years, and remains to this day one of the Templars' most enigmatic relics.*

Opposite top The enigmatic panel painting. The identity of the subject is unknown – the head of Christ perhaps, or John the Baptist.
Opposite bottom The interior looking east. The panel painting is visible to the right.
Below St Mary's Church, Templecombe, from the south.

That cottage had once been the home of one of the Templars' chaplains, after Templecombe, their only preceptory in Somerset, had been granted to them by Serlo FitzOdo around 1185. It was the administrative centre for the whole of the West Country, standing on the direct route between the important ports of Bristol and Poole. The Templars' church was St Mary's, about half a mile to the north of the preceptory; it is in this church that the painting, on the original wooden panel, is now displayed.

It is the face of a bearded man, presumably either Christ or John the Baptist. The style and detail of the painting are devotional, but it shows none of the signs of divinity commonly employed at the time, such as a halo or an inscription. Before the painting was taken to the church, it had suffered clumsy attempts to clean it, which resulted only in dimming the original bright colours.

It will probably never be known who secreted the painting, fixing it to the ceiling and plastering over it, but the reason can readily be guessed. At the time of the Templars' suppression, with king's men arresting the brothers and searching every part of their properties, someone wanted to hide this precious object and chose a simple but ingenious way of doing so. Perhaps he never imagined not being able to retrieve it later — certainly he could not have predicted the impact it would have on a later age.

After the suppression of the Templars, their property was as usual passed on to the Hospitallers, who seem to have been able to effectively develop the lands they inherited from the Order in the west. Subsequent centuries saw little change to the church lying quietly in the verdant Vale of Blackmore, until the Second World War when it was damaged by German bombs. As for that outhouse with its long-concealed secret, it was demolished some time after the war, leaving no significant record.

IN SEARCH OF THE KNIGHTS TEMPLAR

There was an attempt more recently, in 1996, to excavate the Templecombe site, when the television show *Time Team* chose it for one of its three-day whirlwind digs. On the first day, some evidence of Templar buildings was found, so the team pressed ahead with enthusiasm. Unfortunately they were making an erroneous presumption about where the buildings were. And it was only on the third day, when they consulted the tithe map that indicates monastic land, that the error was discovered—by which time it was too late.

Their loss was our loss; modern excavations at Templar sites are rare, South Witham being the only other major dig. The excavation here at Templecombe might have been able to augment that, had the television team managed to survey the correct area. Perhaps in the future an excavation will take place at a Templars' site, either here or elsewhere, which will reveal and preserve their buildings for all to see.

✝ THE TEMPLECOMBE PAINTING is sited just inside the entrance to the church, on the south wall. The panel has hinge marks, indicating that it might have been used as a door, possibly of a reliquary or a cupboard. It has recently been carbon-dated to 1280, making it contemporary with the Templecombe preceptory.

The cryptic nature of the painting has inevitably fuelled much debate as to its purpose and meaning to the Templars, focusing chiefly on two areas — one Christian, one pagan: the painting's resemblance to the Turin Shroud, and the Templars' alleged worship of 'heads'.

The head portrayed in the Templecombe painting is remarkably similar

to that on the shroud — the cloth imprinted with the image of a man's body, purportedly that of the crucified Christ when he was prepared for burial. This has led to claims that at one time the Templars held the relic, having gained possession of it during the Sack of Constantinople by the crusading army in 1204. They would then be in a position to copy from it.

It is known that a relic called the 'Mandylion' was kept at Constantinople around the year 1000, as there was a record of a previous ransom. The Mandylion may have been the shroud itself or 'Veronica's Veil'. Veronica was the saint who during Christ's journey towards his crucifixion offered him her veil to wipe his face. After he did so, his likeness remained on the

Above The Mandylion, or St Veronica's veil, retaining the image of Christ after he had used it to wipe his face on the way to his crucifixion.

Opposite top left Detail of a Celtic cauldron, the Aylesford Pail, from Kent, probably for ritual use. The inclusion of a head marks the convergence of the two pagan beliefs of head worship and the magic cauldron, all later to be absorbed into Christian tradition into the Holy Grail.

Opposite top right Another Celtic head, on this occasion Templar, from Carran Templars, chapel, County Clare, Ireland.

cloth, and Veronica took it to Rome. This cloth became an orthodox Christian relic, commonly featuring in devotional paintings.

The Templecombe painting may be a representation of this veil — the border gives it a similarity to other examples.

It has been suggested that Veronica's Veil and the Turin Shroud are the same object — the shroud being kept folded with just the face on display.

The shroud has generated controversy for centuries: authentic holy relic or medieval fake? As yet, modern scientific analysis has not been conclusive.

The Templecombe painting's other link to the Templars takes them away from orthodox Christian relics to pagan images. At their trial, they were accused of worshipping 'heads', which were described as being bearded, occasionally taking the form of a two- or three-dimensional 'idol'. Addison cites the evidence given by John de Donyngton, an ex-Templar, now a member of the Minorites monastic order: in relation to 'head-worshipping', he had heard that the Templars were in possession of four such idols, one in London, one at Temple Bruer, one at Bisham and a fourth at a place north of

IN SEARCH OF THE KNIGHTS TEMPLAR

the Humber. Another Minorite, John Waleby de Bust, said he had heard the Templars kept a 'gilded head' in a secret location at the Temple in London (see page 54). It should be noted that none of these witnesses would commit themselves, and had always 'heard that...' Possibly they were frightened by the Templars, or were motivated by inter-monastic rivalries.

It may well be that what were perceived as 'heads' did indeed exist but were in fact innocent images and artefacts—all Templar churches had many images and carvings, such as the 'green man', which could be considered pagan but would have had a different implication for the Templars.

The allegation of head-worship perhaps has its root in the memory of Druids and pagan rites. Celts revered heads, which were said to bring prosperity, and decorated their pillars with carved skulls—the Romans described them as 'head hunters'. The practice of carving a head into a wall comes from this Celtic influence.

According to legend, the head of the ancient Celtic hero, Bran, was by his dying command cut off and buried in London at the 'white hill' facing France so that no harm should come to the country. This white hill is assumed to be Tower Hill, and Bran's cult seems to have been maintained because of his Gaelic name, Branduibh ('bran' meaning raven, and 'duibh' meaning black)—it is said to this day that if the ravens leave the Tower, England will suffer. The presence of a Templars' altar in a crypt close by gives

Below The 'Green Man', the nature symbol of rebirth and fertility, tracing a spiral path through time, being reborn every year and yet slowly evolving with each birth. This example is a misericord from St Lawrence's Church, Ludlow.

further pause for thought. (See the entries on All Hallows and the Tower of London, pages 52 and 64.)

And of course the Templars' favourite, the 'green man', is a clear link with the heads of the Celts, which were said to make the land fertile.

The head that the Templars were alleged to worship has acquired the name 'Baphomet'. By far the most likely origin of this world is from a corruption of the medieval French version of Mohammed. Peter Partner

states that one of the old French names for Mohammed was in fact Baphomet, so in this case no corruption would have been involved.

The story of Bran and his magic head dovetails into a much more potent legend: the Holy Grail, signified by the name of the Grail Castle, where the grail is first encountered in the form of a dish or 'graal'. The castle is called 'Corbinec' or 'Corbin'— *corbin* is an old French word meaning 'raven'.

At the start of the legend Bran has a cauldron, which is said to restore the dead to life. After the Irish king asks for Bran's sister's hand in marriage, Bran presents him with the cauldron. Unfortunately, war breaks out and the cauldron is used to regenerate the hostile armies from Ireland, the soldiers being boiled back to life in the cauldron overnight. The loss of the cauldron spells the end for Bran's mortal existence, and his head then becomes the protection of England.

Above Detail of the Gundestrup Bowl, depicting Cernunnos, the Celtic 'green man' and god of fertility.
Right Templar horned 'green man' from St Michael's in Garway.

Templars were Normans who were originally Vikings, with many real and legendary cauldrons of their own. The Gundestrup Bowl is a ritual vessel found in a dried peat bog at Raevmose in Jutland, probably left there as an offering. On its surface is depicted the pagan god Cernunnos, the horned god that has possible Templar connections. The 'green man' at the Templar church at Garway (see page 200) is said to be a representation of Cernunnos.

Cauldrons and vessels are usually mythically connected with sustenance, both literal and mystical. They provide food and, like Bran's, are sometimes able to conquer death. 'Wherever it was there were good things in abundance. Whoever looked upon it even though he was sick unto death, could not die that week; whoever looked at it continually, his cheeks never grew pale nor his hair grey' (quoted by H.A. Guerber in *Myths and Legends of the Middle Ages*).

It seems, though, that by the time of the Templars all these cauldrons had evolved within Christian tradition into one object: 'the Holy Grail'. This is part of a common process: many Christian elements can be found in pre-Christian paganism — so many, in fact, that the medieval church claimed that the devil had gone back in time and inserted evidence that would later undermine Christianity. As an actual relic of the Passion, the Grail did not feature in the early accounts, which do include the True Cross and the Spear of Longinus that pierced the side of Christ. No early crusader would have thought of searching for the Grail in the Holy Land, as it was not part of the Christian catalogue of possible relics. The Grail appears to have originated from the pagan legends. So the later tradition would have Joseph of Arimathea, who buried the body of Christ in his own tomb, travelling to England with the Grail, about thirty years after Christ's death, to build the first Christian church in Britain at Glastonbury.

It seems apt that the nearest Templar preceptory to Glastonbury should be Templecombe, with its own enigmatic Grail associations.

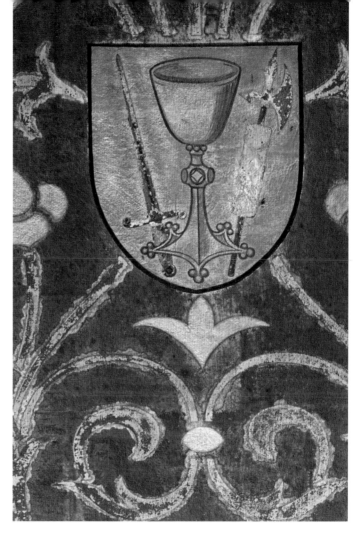

Above The spear and chalice, symbols of fertility subsumed into the Christian iconography. Their shapes also give the letters I and O, included in the ancient name for God: IAO. The shapes are found on the Gundestrup Bowl (opposite) – the round torque being 'O', the snake 'I'.

✠ TEMPLE

(CORNWALL) An ancient land, far from civilisation—a desolate land, since the time of the Romans the refuge for tribes and clans at war with invaders from the east. The moors of England's far west were the most remote of outposts for the Templars, in an age when true wilderness still existed. They made their mark here as they did everywhere, though much of their presence has been erased by time and the knights lie in unmarked graves. The church they founded outlived them, only to fall into ruin before being reborn.

The Templars controlled most of what was later renamed Bodmin Moor. In their time, the land was named after them—'Temple Moor'. It gained a dark reputation, which led to a local saying: 'Send him/her to Temple Moor', implying the person (most likely a pregnant girl) should disappear and be seen no more. Even by the nineteenth century, a guide to Cornwall referred to a 'desert heath, called Temple Moor; truly, a waste, howling wilderness'. And the small village of Temple was in the centre of it. With no roads—the Romans' road-building did not reach this far—the village was effectively isolated, and seems to have had a similar reputation to the moor. According to a local anecdote, the entire male population of Temple were once hanged for sheep stealing—though they turn out to be the two men who comprised the entire male population.

No archaeological excavations have been undertaken around the village, and the extent of the Templars' buildings is unclear. There is a suggestion that their main manor was north of the church, somewhere around the present houses and farm. They built their church, dedicated to St Catherine of Alexandria, some time during the twelfth century.

The Templars may have had another preceptory, in Trebeigh, further south, though records are unclear. George Tull suggests it was indeed a full

Right St Catherine's Church in Temple, from the west.
Opposite top St Michael's Mount, Cornwall, a mystical destination for pilgrims since prehistory.
Opposite bottom The last remnant of the preceptory of Trebeigh, a solitary cross in the churchyard of St Ivo, St Ive in Cornwall.

IN SEARCH OF THE KNIGHTS TEMPLAR

Templar preceptory, which would in due course be handed over to the Hospitallers. However, a very detailed and painstaking paper compiled in 1953 by W.D.J. Cargill (*The Knights Hospitaller and their Preceptory of Trebeigh in Cornwall*) makes it fairly certain that Trebeigh belonged to the Hospitallers throughout. Cargill also gives some colourful local background, describing the holy spring nearby and the farmers who continue to complain about the stones from the 'knights' house' that blunt their ploughs. There are also legends of tunnels that run from the preceptory site to the church, where the 'knights stored their treasure.'

Members of the local Old Cornwall Society have concurred with Tull, rescuing an ancient cross from the Trebeigh preceptory and erecting it on the south side of St Ivo's Church in the nearby village of St Ive. The modern plinth below the old cross reads: 'This stone represents the historic link with the Knights Templars and Hospitallers who held the advowson of the parish and the preceptory of Trebeigh 1150–1540.'

Whatever the true extent of their holdings in Cornwall, the Templars did what they always did and worked the land in the most effective way to generate profit for the Order. Here, money was in sheep and fisheries, and probably tin-mining. Another role reflected the reason for their original foundation: protecting pilgrims. Many pilgrims would come this way to visit the mystical site of St Michael's Mount near Penzance. Traders and travellers would have used this route too — rather than risking a hazardous coastal voyage around Land's End, they could cut across the moor from the ports of north Cornwall to Fowey, an important embarkation point for Europe. As well as

protection, the Templars could offer accommodation— a refuge in this stretch of wild and lawless land.

To guide travellers on their way, they would follow the traditions maintained since prehistoric times and put up stone markers. These so-called Cornish crosses, erected in their own distinct fashion by many of the monastic settlements in the area, varied in style from standing stones fashioned into a cross shape, to those in which a cross is carved into the head of the stone.

The similarity of some of the 'wheel-headed' crosses to the cross pattée of the Templars is striking. And indeed the crosses found around this part of Bodmin Moor are more like Templar crosses than those in other areas.

Many of the crosses seen today have been moved from their original locations and so it is difficult to assess their function. Two examples of Templar-style wheel-headed crosses can be found in the nearby village of Blisland, which has the sister church to the one at Temple, dedicated to SS Protus and Hyacinth. It is worth a visit—the interior has been preserved and in some areas restored to its pre-Reformation state, including an ornate rood screen.

One cross, which is damaged, can be found at the back of the west side of the churchyard, almost in the hedge—re-erected here after being discovered in a wall of the church during repair work. Whether the cross was put into the wall as an act of absorbing its 'power', or whether it was just convenient building material, is unknown. The cross stands on a plinth, which has the enigmatic inscription (now almost illegible): 'Unknown yet well known.'

The second cross, identical to the other but in better condition, stands by the side of the road just outside the village, by a well.

Once the Templars left the area, their church in Temple gained a peculiar notoriety. Their freedom from local parish control was not rescinded on their suppression and, unusually, it survived to allow instant marriages. Like

an English Gretna Green, it required no banns to be read or licence to be obtained, and so had the dubious power to marry whoever turned up. As the local priests carried out these independent unions, the unsavoury reputation of the church grew.

The writer John Norden, in 1584, described Temple church as 'a lawless church where many bad marriages are consummated and where are wonte to be buried such as wrought violent death upon themselves'. Carew describes the church, 'lying in a wild wastrel, exempt from the bishop's jurisdiction, as once appertaining to the Templars ... [where] many a bad marriage bargain is there yearly slubbered up'.

The church continued to have a troubled history before it was eventually abandoned—remaining in a ruinous state until one night it collapsed altogether in one of the frequent gales. Its murky reputation persisted even in its demise, when the body of a local tramp was found in the rubble, killed as he took shelter from the storm.

All that was left standing of the church was the arch that supported the bell tower. In 1883 a fund of £33 was established for restoration work; this retained the remaining arch and kept to the original design. The unmarked Templar graves were left lying in ground that is now grown over.

On May Day 1883 the Temple church bells rang out across the moor for the first time in over a hundred years, when the Bishop of Truro, Dr Benson, who later became the Archbishop of Canterbury, consecrated the new church.

While the church regained its respectability, the landscape continued to inspire stories of wild romance and mystery, typified perhaps by Daphne du Maurier's *Jamaica Inn*. There are echoes of older tales, too—a few miles to the southwest lies Dozemary Pool, the legendary home of the Arthurian 'Lady of the Lake'.

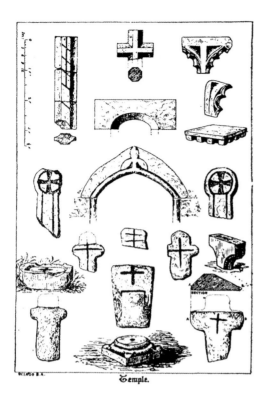

Temple.

Above A drawing of stones found in the ruins of the Templars' original church. Most of these are now sealed into the outhouse wall.

Opposite top left Templar cross at the end of the handrail.

Opposite top right The outhouse wall containing the original Templar stones.

Opposite middle left The original piscina now sealed into the outhouse wall.

Opposite middle St Catherine in the western window of the church.

Opposite middle right A window of the tower showing a Templar knight.

Opposite bottom left The arch leading into the tower is the only feature that was left standing after the original Templar church collapsed in a gale.

Opposite bottom right A Templar cross from the east window.

✠ THERE IS NO SUGGESTION now of the church's earlier history—the site as a whole has a very peaceful atmosphere. Fresh flowers are collected daily and put into the church, where children often leave evidence of school projects.

A small iron gate marks the entrance, and through this the church is reached down a path that descends through the churchyard. The church has recently received a grant to assist in its upkeep and the iron railing to the right is evidence of this, bearing the Templar cross at each end.

By the church is an outbuilding, which has been partly constructed using decorative stones from the old Templar buildings. At the gable ends are two stone crosses, mounted on bases.

Set into its north wall is a selection of crosses and the old piscina. These crosses are similar to ones seen around Cornwall. In his *Pagan Origins of Cornish Crosses*, R.A. Courtney suggests that many were originally Neolithic standing stones that have been Christianised, first by etching a cross into their surface, and then later shaping them. This practice of conversion is most prevalent in Brittany, where many of the large menhirs have a cross carved into the top. Brittany was converted to Christianity from Wales via Cornwall, and the tradition of transforming the crosses may have been introduced at the same time.

The church is accessed through the south porch. Above the door within the porch is mounted the base of the original font; below this, carved into the stone, there is what appears to be a floral design.

The font stands to the left of the entrance; the bell tower is beyond this. The arch supporting the bell tower remains from the original building.

Beyond this is the stained-glass representation of St Catherine, who was favoured by the Templars.

High up at either side of the tower are two more stained-glass windows: the right depicting a Templar on horseback and the left St Luke—there is a local belief that a Templar chapel dedicated to him stood nearby. Beneath this pane is a Templar cross, but this is not visible from the ground and the inquisitive visitor may need to stand on a chair to be able to view it.

The eastern end of this small church has two stained-glass windows depicting Jesus and the disciples and a nativity scene, a gift from a Colonel Goldsworthy. Above these two windows is a circular window depicting the Templar cross flanked by the signs for alpha and omega.

To the left of the altar is a small transept containing the visitors' book and further information about the site.

IN SEARCH OF THE KNIGHTS TEMPLAR

THE MIDLANDS

A MAJOR TEMPLAR PRECEPTORY in the Midlands was Temple Balsall, in Warwickshire. Remnants of the original timber-framed hall survive, though encased in red brick; what is accessible is the 'cathedral in the forest' of Arden. This spacious church, dedicated to St Mary the Virgin, is a fine example not only of Templar architecture, but also of the phenomenon whereby the Order would build a large, handsome church commensurate with the prevailing importance of the site, which would then dwindle, leaving the church incongruously dominant in a small village. ✛ Two other preceptories were significant in their day and, oddly, shared a common fate in modern times. At Rothley in Leicestershire, only the original chapel survives, while the site is now occupied by a hotel. Another hotel, in Sandford, Oxfordshire, incorporates elements of the old preceptory here in its fabric — it could be said that both of these establishments are carrying on the tradition of monastic hospitality. ✛ An even more unusual Templar building is in Cambridgeshire — Denny Abbey, the only surviving 'hospital' of the Order in England. It was dedicated to the welfare of those knights who were too old or too infirm to fight in the Holy Land, and who found themselves leaving the heat and dust of the East to live out their days in the chilly mists of the fen country. Denny existed in partnership with Great Wilbraham, which functioned rather like a 'satellite', supplying food for the elderly residents; it was never a full preceptory itself, but of its buildings the original flint church has survived. ✛ A third site in Cambridgeshire associated with the Templars is in the city of Cambridge itself, the so-called Round Church. Of uncertain date and provenance, this may have even pre-dated the Templars, being built by a mysterious earlier order that then vanished from history. ✛

✝ CAMBRIDGE ROUND CHURCH

The Church of the Holy Sepulchre in the city of Cambridge is, appropriately, commonly known as the Round Church, and is probably the oldest surviving example of the medieval round church in Britain—only four remain. With the Templars' penchant for such churches, it is popularly attributed to them, but there is no unequivocal record of them building it, or owning it. What makes it important is its close resemblance to the round churches known to have belonged to the Order. These are now lost, so Cambridge's Round Church provides an invaluable guide to early, Romanesque Templar architecture.

Previous page
Romanesque zigzag carving on the arches above the solid Norman pillars of Cambridge Round Church.
Opposite above The tower of the Round Church from the southwest.
Opposite below The Round Church from the west looking across Bridge Street.
Below An old print of the Round Church.

The round nave, with its eight thick, round Norman pillars, is very close to the early Templar round churches such as Temple Bruer, Holborn and Garway, all of which now have no more than traces of the nave. The other surviving round churches are at London's Temple, the Holy Sepulchre, Northhampton and the Hospitallers' Little Maplestead. If Cambridge's church really was built by the Templars, then it would surely have been the first ever. The site, now at the junction of St John's Street and Sidney Street, was granted by Abbot Reinald of Ramsey some time between 1114 and 1130 to members of the 'Fraternity of the Holy Sepulchre', who evidently dedicated the church accordingly. Strangely, there is nothing more known of this order—it vanished from history. But if the earlier date of the gift of land is correct, then this would have been fourteen years before Hugh de Payens, the founder of the Templars, arrived in Britain.

Perhaps after building their church, members of the Fraternity became absorbed into either the Templars or the Hospitallers. In any case, some time after its foundation, the Church of the Holy Sepulchre became a parish church serviced by the Austin Friars from the nearby Hospital of St John (which later became St John's College).

By the eighteenth century, the church—like so many others of its time— had fallen into disrepair and started to collapse. It was restored in the 1840s by the Camden Society, which had been founded in 1839 at Cambridge. This was a group concerned with the 'authenticity' of church architecture, part of the Gothic Revival that created modern buildings such as London's St Pancras Station and the Natural History Museum. Their vision was to return churches to their simple original form, and, luckily, their restoration of Cambridge's Round Church is viewed as being very authentic. They were also to work very effectively on the fabric of Temple Balsall (see page 142). It is difficult—though an interesting exercise—to assess just what is original and what is early Victorian restoration.

The group could become excessive in their pursuit of 'purity', especially where interiors were concerned. They evidently equated purity with austerity, eschewing decoration as vulgar—a view that persists to this day. But in fact

the internal pillars and arches here would originally have been brightly, even garishly, painted, just like original Greek temples and statuary.

The 1900 edition of the local *Kelly's Directory* has an admirably succinct description of the church, still accurate after more than a century:

> [It] consists of the circular portion, which forms the principal entrance to the church, chancel with aisles and an octagonal embattled turret on the north side containing 2 bells: the round part is constructed of large stones, carefully squared, and has a good Norman doorway enriched with zigzag ornament: the interior displays a circular arcade of eight short but massive columns without bases, supporting a clerestory from which springs a vaulted conical roof: since 1845 the church has been restored by the Camden Society, and the Perpendicular insertions replaced by windows in the Norman style, the embattled tower, which had been reared above the circular clerestory, removed, a bell turret erected and the eastern part rebuilt: the east window is stained ...

Poignantly, the only verifiable contact the Templars had with Cambridge is after their arrest, when they were brought from the surrounding countryside to be held at Cambridge Castle — which is now just a mound of earth.

IN SEARCH OF THE KNIGHTS TEMPLAR

Opposite above Some of these carvings are original and some restored – it's not clear which are which. The overall effect is one of simple beauty.
Opposite bottom left The gallery of the round nave.
Opposite bottom right The octagonal design, with eight supporting pillars, based on the Church of the Holy Sepulchre in Jerusalem.
Left The Round Church from the north.
Top left The fifteenth-century east extension.

Top right Detail of floor tiles from the round nave.
Above left The massive pillars of the round nave. The need for this sturdy support is a feature of churches that pre-date the Gothic building style of the twelfth century, when internal support was replaced by the external support of buttressing.
Above centre The west porch still retains the fine Romanesque carving.
Above right The symbols on the vaulting echo the design of the floor tiles.

✚ DENNY ABBEY

(CAMBRIDGESHIRE) *When a knight's fighting life came to an end through age or infirmity, he would often go home to the land of his birth and find refuge in one of the Order's 'hospitals'—a term still used today for the Royal Hospital in Chelsea, devoted to the welfare of ex-soldiers. An English knight retired from years of active service could leave the dusty heat of the Holy Land for the biting winds and eerie mists of the Cambridgeshire fens, where Denny Abbey carried on the monastic tradition of caring for the sick and the elderly, in this case the Templars themselves.*

Opposite top and middle The abbey from the east, showing the original pre-Templars arch – the internal arch leading on to the altar, which would have been around where the present-day notice board is.
Opposite bottom Denny Abbey from the north.
Below Denny Abbey from the south. The blocked-up door at the top right led on to the garderobe, a medieval toilet and the origin of the word 'wardrobe'. The dual meaning comes from the practice of hanging up clothes above the cesspit, where ammonia from the waste would kill bugs infesting them.
Below right The Templars' west door.

Denny is one of the two known hospitals for the Order in England, the other being at Eagle near Lincoln. As Evelyn Lord notes, the hospital at Denny apparently enjoyed the benefit of glazed windows, keeping out the bitter fenland winds. Found at the site was a glass urinal—an essential diagnostic tool used at the time to assess the appearance, smell and taste. The master here was known as Custos Infirmorum, and he may have had specialist medical training.

When the site was excavated, Templar graves contained bones with evidence of degenerative diseases, arthritic conditions that may have developed through hardship and the repetitive training a knight had to endure. The occupant of the grave outside the west door had a more unusual claim to fame: as the comprehensive and informative guidebook points out, he had been buried with a 'pewter chalice and an unusual round lead disc marked with a geometric cross'; he was probably a Templar priest.

The first structure on the site was a church built by monks of the Benedictine Order, who started work in 1159. In 1170 they passed it on to the Templars. The background to this transaction is unclear, but it may have been in payment for an outstanding debt. Denny then became the first recorded Templar establishment in Cambridgeshire.

At the same time they laid the foundations for a preceptory at Great Wilbraham (see page 134), about ten miles to the south. Wilbraham functioned partly to provide the residents at Denny with fresh food; in return Denny provided 40 shillings a year for the upkeep of a priest. This arrangement was maintained throughout the life of the Order, even though in time Denny seems to have become more productive.

When they took over the Benedictines' church, the Templars set about adding to it and building what was to be the hospital cum retirement home for elderly knights. The church itself was primarily a place of worship for the Order, and the Templars built extensively elsewhere on the site to provide essential services. This must have been a challenging task for the new incumbents—draining an area of marsh and islands, below sea level, and making their estate as self-sufficient as possible.

Above The refectory, which stands to the north of the abbey. Recently used as a barn, and now with the addition of a modern roof.

Above right The inlaid floor of the refectory.

Opposite top Carved capitals on the south door of the Templars' church, now an internal arch.

Opposite middle left A strange corbel, a 'goggle-eyed' nun from the internal arch.

Opposite right A bearded head from a first-floor alcove, probably Templar, which invites immediate comparison with other Templar heads such as that on the Templecombe panel (see page 110).

Opposite bottom left A lion carved into the stone of a first-floor alcove.

That the brothers here lived the requisite simple life of monks was proved by the inventory of 1308, after their arrest. The only valuables were found in the chapel—some silver chalices, bowls and silk cloth. The abbey was described as having an 'extensive library', but at the time this may have meant no more than a few books.

Of the elderly knights arrested at Denny, one was insane and two were crippled; in total they were not more than a dozen. They remained in Cambridge Castle until 30 September 1309, when, with the exception of William de Mawringges who had died meanwhile, they were handed over to the Constable of the Tower of London.

When the surviving (and mentally able) Cambridge brethren were examined, the preceptor of Denny, William de la Forde, said he had been a Templar for forty-two years and seen as many as a hundred brothers admitted into the Order. One of the members from Denny, Robert the Scot, had actually been a Templar twice. He had first been admitted in Syria, twenty-six years earlier, but afterwards left and was outside the Order for two years. Wishing to rejoin, he went to Rome for confession and absolution; this granted, he gratefully resumed Templar life at Nicosia in Cyprus. Given that he testified that he had seen no admissions in England, it is likely that he had only recently retired from active service.

Due to their infirmity, the remaining Templars from Denny were allowed to do penance at All Hallows Church, close to the Tower of London where they were being held. They were then returned to the fens and were admitted into various local religious houses.

The Hospitallers took over at Great Wilbraham, but they did not seem interested in developing Denny, even though they had the right to take possession of it, as all other Templar properties. The buildings were acquired by Mary de Valence, Countess of Pembroke (and founder of Pembroke College, Cambridge). She moved in an order of Franciscan nuns, the 'Poor Clares', from Waterbeach, who occupied the site until the Dissolution, upon which the abbey was used as a farmhouse. It was to stay as such until the 1960s, providing eight centuries of continuous occupation, all of which left their traces—the initial religious architecture superseded by practical changes such as a range oven and progressively smaller doors.

Since 1997, Denny Abbey has functioned as a 'farmland museum', housing an evocative collection of old farming tools and machinery—a distant echo of the Templars' original industry and enterprise.

Above The first floor, looking west. The wall on the right would have been the external south wall of the Templars' church.
Right The Templar south entrance containing Romanesque capitals; it would have led from the church to the grounds.

IN SEARCH OF THE KNIGHTS TEMPLAR

✠ IT IS WORTH taking the time to explore the site as a whole, including the grounds, which contain traces of lost Templar outbuildings now indicated by earthworks. There are also medieval timbered barns similar to those at Cressing (page 86), though on a smaller scale. Under the lawn to the east lie the foundations of the eastern part of the original church; the remains of the transepts and nave survive within the main building. In common with some other Templar churches and chapels, the alignment is not exactly east–west but a little to the north of east (this phenomenon is discussed further in the Appendix, page 242).

Above left Ground floor of the eastern wing looking south.
Above right The Countess of Pembroke's rooms on the first floor. The countess, Mary de Valence, was the owner and founder of the convent. She also founded Pembroke College, Cambridge.
Left Graffiti from the Countess of Pembroke's rooms.

✚ GREAT WILBRAHAM

(CAMBRIDGESHIRE) *The Templars' settlement here was on a small scale, never to be a full preceptory—they were granted a manor house and church at around the same time as Denny Abbey was founded. In fact Great Wilbraham functioned more as a satellite of Denny, the Order's hospital that looked after aged and infirm brothers, supplying the veterans with fresh food from the local dairy and sheep farms (which were also the source of particularly high quality wool). The manor house is long gone, but the spacious flint church remains, set in a picturesque Cambridgeshire village.*

The Templar household here would have comprised just a preceptor (despite there being no actual preceptory), a priest and a brother, who managed the estate and employed local tenants to work the farms, and also the two water-mills and a windmill. In exchange for the food they supplied to Denny, they received 40 shillings a year to help pay for the priest.

The *History of the County of Cambridge* describes their establishment:

> The house of the preceptory seems to have been a small manor house, very simply furnished, and the only ornaments of the chapel were a vestment, with towels, worth a mark, and one silver chalice, together with the necessary books: in the chest, for transmission to the master, was £4. The most elaborate fittings in the house seem to have been those for dairying, with presses for cheese, a churn, a large fixed cauldron for heating milk, and other utensils.

The manor house had been given to the Templars in 1226 by a Peter Malauney. The church, dedicated to St Nicholas, also dates from the thirteenth century; it was either built entirely by the Templars, or developed from a pre-existing Saxon church.

After the suppression, the Hospitallers took possession in 1313, just one year later. This must have been one of the first properties they inherited from the Templars—in most cases it took years of wrangling with the Crown or local landowners to acquire the land and properties.

Opposite top left
Weathered capitals on the arch of the south door.

Opposite top right
Looking east from the Norman font, the church is spacious, consistent with the wealth of the Templars.

Below left The church of St Nicholas from the southeast. Note the blocked-up arch visible on the south transept wall. This is thought to have led on to a private Templar chapel.

Below right The interior looking east. Note the painting on the arches and the shields painted above the far arch.

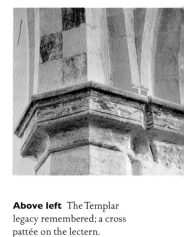

Above left The Templar legacy remembered; a cross pattée on the lectern.

Above middle The altar of the Templar church of St Nicholas.

Above right Detail of chequerboard design on arch.

Far left Interior of south transept. The blocked-up arch is said to have led to the Templars' private chapel. The exterior of the arch is pictured opposite left.

Left The chequer pattern on the arches, the faint remains of a lost tradition. Originally the interior surfaces of the church would have being covered with colourful wall paintings and designs.

✛ ROTHLEY

(LEICESTERSHIRE) The preceptory at Rothley was built on the site of a Roman villa, eventually including large amounts of land, several mills and five dependent chapels. The rent received from Rothley's mills was set aside for a specific purpose: to provide food on special occasions to the Templar knights on duty in the stronghold of Acre—a small but telling demonstration of the role of these preceptories in supporting the Order in the Holy Land. While the original chapel survives, the old manor house vanished long ago. A hotel now standing on the site provides food rather more directly.

As with the other Templar buildings or sites in England that are now used as hotels, the Angel in Grantham and the Four Pillars in Sandford, modern times have been kind to the Templars' heritage here, restoration and refurbishment generally respecting their historic integrity. The old chapel, dating from around 1240, is attached to the north end of Rothley Court Hotel and is largely unaltered; like many other Templar churches and chapels, the alignment is a few degrees to the north of east (see Appendix, page 242).

The Templars already had a house in the city of Leicester before being granted land at Rothley by John de Harecourt in 1203, and the manor house by Henry III in 1228. At its greatest, the preceptory would have comprised, in addition to the chapel and hall, a dormitory, stables, kitchen, storehouses, bakery, buttery and brewery. In 1285 the Order was granted the right to hold a weekly market and annual fair in the village.

✛ THE KEY TO THE CHAPEL is available from the hotel reception.

Above One of two tapestries that hang on the west wall of the chapel. Both show romantic views of Templar life; this one actually has Rothley Chapel in the background.
Right The hotel with its modern Templar parking shields. The chapel is the building to the right.
Above right The simple design of the chapel can be better appreciated when viewed as a separate structure from the main hotel.

IN SEARCH OF THE KNIGHTS TEMPLAR

Top left The splendid interior of Rothley Chapel remembers the founding Templars through banners and shields.

Above left The corbel from the porch.

Above middle Graffiti carved in the porch.

Left Wooden beams in the roof of the chapel.

Top right Detail of a coat of arms on the north wall.

Right middle The double piscina found next to the altar at the east end of the south wall.

Above right This weathered tomb lid, broken in three places, can be found to the left of the altar. The owner is not known.

✝ SANDFORD

(OXFORDSHIRE) *By the time the Templars built their preceptory here, on the banks of the Thames, they were already well set up in the county, having acquired rich properties from a succession of generous patrons. It was during this time that the Templars established the houses that were to develop into the framework of preceptories throughout Britain. Sandford would be their chief preceptory in Oxfordshire, and the only one with significant remains that survive to this day, incorporated within farm buildings now converted into a hotel.*

The Templars had one of their first properties at Oxford, granted during the long civil war between King Stephen and the Empress Matilda (Maud), rival claimants to the English throne—a conflict that tore the country apart until 1153, with the final recognition of Stephen as king, to be succeeded by Matilda's son, the future Henry II.

King Stephen's queen, another Matilda, bestowed the knights with the land she owned at Cowley, in 1131. Ten years later, the Empress Matilda gave the knights the right to keep their animals in Shotover Forest—a rare direct donation from the empress, although her supporters made several contributions.

Robert de Sandford gave his gift of land at Sandford on Thames in 1239, prompting the Templars to decant their preceptory at Cowley to Sandford, two miles to the south. According to George Tull, Robert actually became a Templar later in life.

The land around the Thames at Sandford was fairly marshy, with areas above ground becoming small islands; cattle could be ferried to and fro on rafts, the islands providing a natural enclosure. The terrain was dangerous, though—nearby Sandford Pool is a mysterious place where many people have drowned, among them five undergraduates from Christ Church.

Right View of the hotel from the east, including the old barn on the left, with filled-in windows, which was the Templars' chapel. The house on the right is on the site of the Templars' manor.
Opposite top The main house at Sandford, until recently a farmhouse, now a hotel. Built over the site of the Templars' manor.
Opposite right A rare original Templar cross from the preceptory, now located above the door of the main house, visible in the photograph opposite top.
Opposite left Coat of arms on the west wall of the main house.

IN SEARCH OF THE KNIGHTS TEMPLAR

When the Templars were arrested in 1307, the preceptor of Sandford was William Sautre, who, as the *History of the County of Oxford* records, would be one of the principal witnesses at the trial. One of the Sandford brothers was Richard de Colingham, who had been there for the past six years. According to the *History*, Richard spoke on the subject of the mystic girdles which the brethren were said to wear, saying that they used certain belts called 'girdles of chastity'. These ropes were mentioned in the trials throughout Europe — many Templars admitted they wore some sort of rope around their waist, next to their skin, but insisted it had no diabolical connotation but the very opposite: it was a permanent reminder of their monastic vow of chastity.

After the suppression, the land and buildings were handed over to the Hospitallers, who were able to maintain and develop the site. In an article for the online *Sandford on Thames Village Magazine*, Jacqueline Smithson notes:

> We can picture the manor of Sandford as it was nearly 500 years ago from a report written in 1512 by Sir Thomas Leland, sent to audit the Hospitallers' lands by their head Prior, Thomas Docwra. Two water-mills are mentioned, together with two fisheries ... There were orchards and dovecotes round the brothers' house, and the land amounted to roughly 250 acres in total.
>
> It is hard to discover exactly when the Hospitallers left their Priory in Sandford, but the Order was finally dissolved in 1541 when, with many others, their Prior refused to accept Henry VIII's claim of royal supremacy over the Pope and the Catholic Church.

The property later became a farm, called Temple Farm, which after some years of deterioration was converted into a hotel, the Four Pillars. As with other Templar properties or sites in England now used as hotels (the Angel at Grantham and Rothley Court in Leicestershire), the restoration has been carried out sensitively, with due regard for the Templars' history.

Above Looking southeast from the preceptory site to the church of St Andrew, which dates from 1100.
Above right The west wall of the main house.
Opposite top left Beams extending down from what is thought to be the Templars' chapel, now the reception area for the hotel.
Opposite top right The north wall of the Templars' chapel, later reused as a barn and now part of the hotel.

IN SEARCH OF THE KNIGHTS TEMPLAR

Above The hotel from St Andrew's Church, rather resembling the Templars' preceptory complex.
Far left The boating gate to the hotel from the Thames. Around this gate, set into the wall, are a number of recovered pieces of decorative stone from the preceptory.
Left Set into the wall by the river gate, a carved number '8'; this has been collected from the remains of the Templars' preceptory and is used as decoration here.

✝ TEMPLE BALSALL

(WARWICKSHIRE) *Deep in the Forest of Arden — the mythical setting for* As You Like It — *stands a Templar church built as part of the preceptory here, almost a cathedral for what is now a tiny village. There is a Shakespeare connection, though — the poet's ancestors came from this area, and would have known the Templars' preceptory at its height, when it was the administrative centre for all the Order's estates in Warwickshire. What remains of the original timber-framed hall survives within a redbrick shell, while written records give a valuable insight into the Templar way of life.*

Shakespeare's provenance is described by Michael Wood in his *In Search of Shakespeare*:

> The Shakespeares' ancestors came from around the village of Balsall with its old chapel and hall of the Knights Templars. Down Green Lane, shrouded by thickets of ash and silver birch, across a ford that runs deep in Winter there is still a red-brick farm house where Adam of Oldeditch lived in the 14th century. His son gave himself the surname Shakespeare. There were still Shakespeares at Oldeditch 100 years later, and almost certainly the clan descended from them.

Coincidentally, William Shakespeare himself was to marry Anne Hathaway in the Templars' church at Temple Grafton.

The manor of Balsall was given to the Templars some time in the 1160s by their long-time and generous supporter, Roger de Mowbray (see page 184). Its name comes from the Anglo-Saxon, a combination of the personal name Baell (or Bele or Bali) and *halh*, meaning a nook or a corner of land.

The hall has some of the few remaining examples of timber aisle pillars, which support the original roof timbers. These timbers have been dated to the late twelfth century, around a hundred years before the church, dedicated to St Mary the

Above William Shakespeare's family came from Temple Balsall – he was to maintain his Templar connections by marrying Anne Hathaway in the nearby church at Temple Grafton. This is a rare photograph of that church, which was demolished in 1875.
Right Temple Balsall church and hall from the west.
Opposite top The church is late twelfth century, built by the Templars and restored in 1845. The chapel would have been one of the last built by the Order before the suppression.

IN SEARCH OF THE KNIGHTS TEMPLAR

Virgin, was built. Its date of around 1290 makes the
church one of the last constructed by the Order before
the suppression, though the figureheads decorating
the exterior may have been taken from earlier chapels.
The church is a high, spacious building, without aisles
or transepts, a style employed by the Templars in some
of their other English churches. As George Tull notes,
this red sandstone church is 'remarkable for the fine
tracery of its windows.'

In common with many other Templar churches and
chapels in the UK, it is aligned slightly to the north of
east, by around 10 degrees (see Appendix, page 242).

Following Templar practice, the brothers would strive to make their estate
here as efficient and productive as possible, which would involve a good
relationship with their tenants. The 'inquest' (inventory) of 1185 spelt out the
reciprocal arrangements:

Above The Templars' Hall
contains the timber frame
of the original Knights' Hall.

THE MIDLANDS : TEMPLE BALSALL

Those at Balsall owe customary dues as follows, 3 days' mowing and 1 day's food will be provided, 3 days' ploughing, 1 day's food provided, 1 day scything and they shall have from the house 1 ram or 8d, 24 loaves and 1 of the best cheeses and a full dish of salt. Colts born on Templars' land may not be sold without the brothers' permission. Daughters cannot be given [in marriage] without the brothers' permission.

As well as abiding by the agreed work/provisions deals, the tenants would also provide a local pool of paid workers, skilled and unskilled, who could be employed when the need arose. The proviso about the disposal of colts and then daughters demonstrates the ownership and control the Templars were able to exert in a feudal system.

The inventory held after the Templars' arrest threw up a rather less common set-up: about half the possessions at Temple Balsall had come from the preceptory at Rothley (see page 136). In her invaluable book *Temple Balsall*, dedicated to a single preceptory, Eileen Gooder suggests that this unusual arrangement was part of the 'clearing up process' following the arrest.

IN SEARCH OF THE KNIGHTS TEMPLAR

The inventory casts an interesting light on the Templars' diet at the time:

57 cheeses (26 from Rothley), 38 sides of bacon (22 from Rothley), two hams, three carcasses, and one quarter of beef (four shoulders of beef from Rothley). 214 hard [salted] fish (108 from Rothley plus 2,200 herrings also from Rothley). Livestock two swans, two peacocks, five geese, 15 capons, two cocks, seven hens, 80 doves.

The inventory also lists numerous 'bushels' of wheat, oats, peas and mixed grains—some of which would have been fodder for livestock. There were the ingredients for brewing beer, the staple drink of the time. Beer was a healthy alternative to plain well water, as the brewing process involved boiling water, which eliminated harmful micro-organisms. In general medieval practice, the brewing ingredients would often be used three times—a method carried on in more recent centuries. The first gave a strong 'man's' brew, similar to the Continental monk's beers available today; the second gave an everyday 'family' brew; and the third a weaker brew for the children, literally 'small beer'.

The preceptory's stock of domestic animals also included 24 plough oxen, 22 bullocks, 33 calves, 65 pigs, 19 piglets and 212 lambs.

As Eileen Gooder points out, the inventory naturally took account of what was there at the time, but, from the Templars' regular stocktaking, it was clear that the amounts fell short of the anticipated totals. The discrepancies, which were effectively written off, were probably the result of opportunistic looting by lay staff employed by the now absent Templars.

Another factor should be considered; forewarned about the impending arrests, many Templars moved out of their

Above A corbel from the south wall, possibly a priest or Templar dignitary. **Left** The extent of the weathering increases the sinister appearance of the figure.
Opposite top High above the nave the carving of a grizzled old knight looks down, clearly displaying the Templars' avoidance of shaving.
Opposite below Weathered corbel from the south wall. The identity of the figure is unknown; the headdress suggests a women or a Saracen.

respective preceptories, discarded their distinctive habits and any other means of identification and travelled to the less accessible areas of the country. And clearly they would need to take as much food as possible.

The Hospitallers managed to get hold of Balsall in 1322. It had been seized in 1314 by John de Mowbray, a descendant of the original donor. This was not an unusual occurrence; descendants of the person who had given property to the Templars often objected to that property then being passed on to another order. Fortunately for the Hospitallers, John supported the rebel Earl of Lancaster against Edward II and, when the rebellion ended unsuccessfully, he was hanged at York, and Balsall was theirs. It remained in their possession until the Dissolution in 1540, after which Henry VIII gave it to his last wife, Catherine Parr.

In later years the church and hall became part of a complex, acquired by Lady Katherine Leveson. As Eileen Gooder records, when she died in 1674 she left all her estates to 'erect and endow a hospital or almshouse for twenty poor women, and a free school for twenty poor boys from Balsall. The minister of the church was to be master of the hospital and teacher to the boys.' In fact the school, almshouses, hall and church all continue to function as intended by Lady Leveson, although the school would appear to accept more pupils than twenty, and not just boys.

The chapel was left to ruin until, starting in 1845, it was restored by George Gilbert Scott. Scott was associated with the Camden Society based in Cambridge, a group who were part of the Gothic Revival and had much to do with the restoration of the Cambridge Round Church (see page 124). Scott also preserved the timbered hall, encasing it in red brick. Overall, his work was sensitive and sympathetic, keeping most of the Templars' structure and making restorations only where needed.

Below left Romantic stained glass from nearby Temple Grafton, showing the Templars and Hospitallers in their caring roles, protecting pilgrims and caring for the sick.

Below right When churches are rebuilt, fonts are usually preserved from the original, and can be the oldest feature. This is the case here; the ancient weathered font with its floral design would have come from the older Templar chapel, utilised in the baptisms of the children born to the workers on the knights' estate.

Above The spacious interior of the church, reflecting Templar wealth.
Left The church and hall have become part of a complex, which was donated by Lady Katherine Leveson, who died in 1674 leaving all her estates to endow almshouses and a free school. These are the almshouses sited to the east of the church.

LINCOLNSHIRE

SOME OF THE LARGEST and most efficient Templar estates in England were concentrated in Lincolnshire; by 1190 the Order controlled some 10,000 acres. The expansive heathlands were ideal not only for grazing sheep — source of the highly lucrative wool trade — but also as training grounds for both men and horses. To this day the landscape bears the marks of their occupation, in the farms named 'Temple', and the fields that still follow the boundaries of their estates. ✠ It was in trade that the Templars initiated a revolution. To maximise profit for their Order, they effectively collectivised local industry: controlling every stage of production and transport, dealing in bulk and benefiting from economies of scale. They were a model of the modern global corporation. ✠ Exactly how many preceptories they built in the county is debatable. Four are generally agreed: Temple Bruer, Willoughton (the largest preceptory built in Britain), South Witham and Aslackby. But opinion regarding Eagle and Mere is divided: Eagle was probably a hospital along the lines of Denny Abbey, and Mere not a full preceptory. ✠ The only extant remains are at Temple Bruer. Nothing now remains of Willoughton and little is known about its structure; but South Witham and Aslackby can be reconstructed through archaeological excavation and old records. Traces of the Templars also exist away from their preceptories — in Lincoln's castle and cathedral, where they were first imprisoned and then tried; and in Grantham's Angel Inn, built by the Templars and continuing as a hotel to this day. In Burton upon Stather a single effigy is a fitting monument to the Order. ✠ The Templars left a less tangible legacy in some of the more superstitious local minds: a reputation for malevolence, which lingered in their old haunts and had to be ritually dispelled. ✠

✚ SOUTH WITHAM

The preceptory here gives a unique insight into the Templar way of life—although no remains are visible above ground. It has the distinction of being the only site so far subjected to a full modern excavation (in 1965–67), providing archaeologists and historians with a detailed, accurate account of the layout of the property and the different stages of building. There is a more readily accessible point of Templar interest in South Witham, in the local church of St John the Baptist, which houses what may be a tangible—if mysterious—link to the old preceptory.

Previous page
Arcading within the tower at Temple Bruer.
Below The River Witham, channelled by the Templars to provide power for their mill.
Bottom Earthworks in the northeast corner of the site, the only remaining evidence of the water mill.

The preceptory site, north of the village in a field appropriately called Temple Hill, provided so much information because the foundations of the original buildings had not actually been changed. By the time the Hospitallers could take possession, the buildings were unfit for habitation and were left to crumble into the ground. Of course, as was usually the case, this process of attrition would have been speeded up by local people taking the old stones for various reasons.

It is not known exactly when the preceptory was founded. Local researcher Peter Ball maintains that it is safe to say only that the founding took place after 1137 and before 1185, the year of the general inquest when an inventory was made of all Templar holdings in England—by this time, South Witham was up and running.

The excavation found that the preceptory was built in three phases. Phase one was the original farm granted to the Templars—a small aisled hall and two outer buildings and a watermill. Phase two was the Templars' own major building, as they demolished the two outer buildings and constructed three major barns similar to those at Cressing (see page 86), as well as animal sheds, gatehouse, guesthouse, chapel, the domestic area—kitchen, bakehouse, brewery/dairy—lesser hall and hall/keep complex. In phase three, in the late thirteenth century, the watermill became redundant after being superseded by a

windmill; the lesser hall was demolished and the great hall enlarged.

The preceptory would have had access to fishponds fed by the River Witham. There were kilns here too, showing evidence of smelting iron and lead.

At South Witham there are the usual legends of Templar tunnels, running from the preceptory to the village. Intriguingly though, Tanyard House, which is sited between the village church and the preceptory, does have a unique cellar —located away from the house, apparently made from part of a tunnel. This particular cellar also has a stone bench on either side with individual seating areas; local historians have suggested that it functioned as a secret chapel.

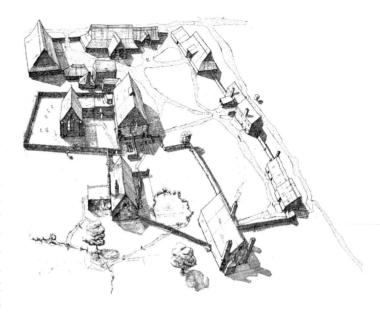

Above The late-thirteenth-century South Witham preceptory as visualised by Jake Goodband.
Below Examples of buckles which were among the many finds of the 1965–67 excavation.

Records show that the Bishop of Lincoln stayed at Witham Temple in 1274, and a royal visit in 1296 would indicate there were Templars here then to receive the distinguished visitor. So the last Templar must have died between the royal visit and the arrest of the knights in 1307.

Following the arrests, the king's keeper took over the running of the site, and records that the preceptory at that time was being administered by Temple Bruer, suggesting that South Witham was in decline before the end of the Order. And it is believed that no knights were then living there— a belief supported by the records of the corrodaries (pensioners) at Temple

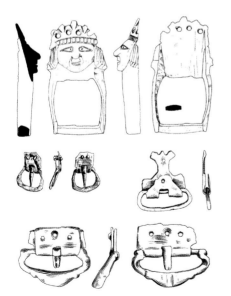

Bruer. A corrody was given to loyal servants when they retired, or in exchange for gifts; it often took the form of board and lodging for the rest of their life. One William Revel gave a gift of land to the knights at South Witham, but he was given his board and lodging at Temple Bruer, suggesting there were no Templars to look after him at South Witham.

The Hospitallers finally gained possession of the site some time between 1312 and 1338, only to find that the buildings were waterlogged and fit only for animals— fortunately for posterity.

In time, more may be learnt from South Witham. Although there are no visible remains above ground on Temple Hill, the site remains a field and as such is available for further archaeological research. In 2001 the South Witham Archaeological Group commenced a feasibility study in regard to further excavations.

✛ THE LOCAL CHURCH of St John the Baptist is cruciform in plan, with a piscina in its north transept that seems to have been set into the wall from another, possibly Templar, chapel. It is known that the Order was part-owner of the church at one time. (Incidentally, there is a pub in the village called the Angel, a common name in Templar areas.)

During the excavation of the preceptory site, in the 1960s, a lidless stone coffin was found in the chapel. In the church here there happens to be a coffin-less lid, which had been used face down for 350 years as a footbridge over the River Witham. In 1905 the rector, the Reverend Steadman Davis, rescued the lid and brought it into the church. It now rests almost hidden

behind the organ. Investigations by the South Witham Archaeological Group suggest that the lid and the now reburied coffin are relatively the same size and—a romantic thought, perhaps—might belong to the last Templar at Witham Temple.

The coffin lid shows a floriated cross similar to Templar examples in Portugal, above which is the ghost-like face of a man. Compared to the detailed carving of the cross, the man's face is quite rudimentary, with eye sockets and curly hair.

The grave slab is unique—which makes it all the more mysterious. F.A. Greenhill's book *Incised Effigial Slabs* describes all the classes of slabs that have been made in Christendom since the Dark Ages, and nowhere is there an example to compare with the one here. The floriated cross is similar to others, but the face—which seems to be attached to the cross as though it were its body—is unique in its appearance and position.

It has been suggested that the 'fins' below the face are the hands of the man clasped in prayer, but this seems unlikely; referring again to Greenhill, no other grave slab can be found with the hands in a position that is anywhere near the one suggested here; and if they are fingers the figure seems to be holding something rather than praying. The object around the neck might be some kind of adornment, possibly eroded to give the appearance of fingers.

Top A carved animal head from the south porch of the church of St John the Baptist.
Above Romanesque piscina in north transept. It may have been brought into the church from the Templars' chapel.

IN SEARCH OF THE KNIGHTS TEMPLAR

Right The church of St John the Baptist from the south.
Below left An intriguing tomb lid from South Witham church. For hundreds of years it lay face down, used as a footbridge over the river. The crude carving of the face contrasts with the detail of the cross.
Right middle The cross on the eastern gable end of the church
Right bottom The Bell Tower, the oldest part of the church, which is thought to date from the eleventh century.

✙ TEMPLE BRUER

The Templars have almost a tangible presence here. The rural site is remote—wild and windy—and has changed little in seven centuries. Uniquely, the ruins have been repaired but not altered or restored, while the location, within a working farm that was named after the original owners, intensifies the authentic atmosphere. Temple Bruer was one of the major preceptories in England, flourishing for over 150 years until the Order fell.

Temple Bruer grew up in the middle of the vast Lincoln Heath, which spread out south of the city. The heath has always been sparsely populated, and in the Templars' time would have been desolate and forbidding. In later centuries, when travel was by stagecoach, it was known as the most hazardous stretch of the journey from London to York. Records show that it was possible to obtain insurance for the whole route—with the exception of the Lincoln Heath run.

In this unprepossessing place, the Templars would with typical vigour and enterprise build their great preceptory and establish a valuable, productive estate. Land was donated to them by local Norman aristocrats from around the mid-twelfth century and throughout the lifetime of the preceptory— whose name, 'Bruer', is derived from the French *bruyère*, meaning heath or heather (highly appropriate for this landscape). As the Templars built up their property, there were rumours of a tunnel running under the heath from the preceptory to the village of Wellingore two miles away—Templar properties were often associated with such clandestine features.

The preceptory would have been walled, and visitors would have required official clearance at the main gate before being allowed entrance. As in all preceptories, it was governed by a preceptor, who may or may not have been a knight. The people living here would fall into one of four

Below The tower of Temple Bruer, part of the preceptory's round church, seen from the southwest across the valley. Most of the other preceptory buildings were located within what is now the field in front of the tower.

IN SEARCH OF THE KNIGHTS TEMPLAR

categories: knights, sergeants, servants and chaplains. In the year 1200 the garrison at Temple Bruer numbered about 150 people, of whom very few would be full knights of the Order.

The Templars built a 'round' church here, one of the eight known in the country: one in Aslackby, south of Temple Bruer; one each in Hereford, Garway, Dover and Bristol; and two in London. It is generally thought that the round churches were built early in the Templars' lifetime.

The village of Temple Bruer did not exist before the Templars came; it was built to house the workforce needed by the Order—labourers, builders and so on—along with their families, who would be the Templars' tenants. In 1259, the village was granted a charter to have a market (originally on Wednesdays but later changed to Fridays).

The original Templar estate extended to the west, to an area known as the Lincoln Cliff, where the knights typically exploited the climate and built a windmill—they were in fact the first recorded users of windmills in Europe. Ermine Street, the old Roman road, runs along the top of the cliff and would have been used by the Templars as they travelled up from London and on to Lincoln and York. It also follows the same route they would have taken to and from their training grounds at Byard's Leap, which marks the southernmost limit of the Templars' property. In a further evocation of past times, the road is still used to exercise horses.

Being answerable only to the pope, the Templars were totally independent of any local requirements or duties. They could fight, pray and raise revenue without recourse to secular authorities, the local clergy, or even the king. Like other preceptories, Temple Bruer was an outpost of what was, in effect, a Templar state, ruled from Jerusalem; its essential role was to generate revenue for the Order to fund its campaigns in the Holy Land.

The Templars' wealth here lay in sheep—huge flocks of them, producing fine quality wool. The wool trade was rapidly expanding to meet an ever-increasing demand, and trade links were developed with Flanders, in the Low Countries, where the wool was processed. The east coast ports of Boston, Grimsby and King's Lynn traded through the Hanseatic League, a confederation of northern European trading states founded in the thirteenth century—a proto Common Market, readily exploited by the Templars, who

Above The eastern end of the church. Beneath this tower and the surrounding land the Reverend Oliver claimed in 1841 that he had found evidence of murder and torture. There are also legends of tunnels – it is said that a tunnel runs under the heath between the tower and the nearby village of Wellingore two miles away.

developed their collectivised method of production and transport.

For instance, all the wool from all the Templar farms in the area was collected at Temple Bruer. It was then shipped in Templar vessels from the eastern ports to the Continent. Because the Templars were involved at every stage of the operation, the system was extremely efficient, and even more economical given the Templars' exemption from tax.

Despite their privileges, it seems that there were limits to the Templars' powers. For instance, they used to hold local tournaments at Byard's Leap until these were mysteriously banned. The official reason for the termination was stated as 'infractions'. Nothing further is known of the matter, though it has been suggested that the ban might have derived from a local, long-running dispute between the Templars and the Ashby family.

> In the early part of the thirteenth century the first recorded dispute between the Templars and the Ashbys arose about the pasturage of 300 sheep on the Heath and this was settled in 1221; but a similar quarrel about the pasturage of 408 sheep, 8 oxen, and 100 hogs, arose about 26 years later, and was only settled in 1247. Even after this date, disputes were not unknown throughout the tenure of the Templars...

The fierce disagreements continued for some two centuries. There is no record of specific incidents, but perhaps this discord influenced the Templars' application for permission to fortify their gatehouse in 1306.

One of the reasons for the lack of clarity surrounding the history of the Order is that few records were kept. The level of literacy among the Templars continues to be hotly debated. The paucity of written records may reflect the fact that the knights, as a military order, held the written word in low esteem. Their job was soldiering and they may have felt that the pen was best left to the purely monastic orders.

Following the suppression of the Order, Temple Bruer was given to the Hospitallers. The Hospitallers made the Templars' house at Mere their commandery, and some of the Templars were allowed to return to Temple Bruer and remain there as pensioners for the rest of their lives. These veterans were the last members of the Templar Order left alive in England. The last Grand Master in Britain, William de la More, had been initiated into the Order at Temple Bruer, and was arrested there. He was the only Templar tried in Britain who refused to admit any heresy and, as a result, he was kept in prison where he apparently died.

The Hospitallers inhabited the site until Henry VIII seized their land and buildings at the time of the Dissolution and presented them to the Duke of Suffolk. Henry himself stayed at the preceptory in 1541 while on a journey to Scotland. Even then the place was reported to be in a ruinous state, and tents had to be erected to provide shelter for the king's entourage. In 1540 a valuation mentioned a 'farm site ... the old "preceptory", with orchards, gardens and houses, a rabbit warren, 2000 acres of sheep ground and a windmill'.

William Stukeley, the seventeenth-century antiquarian, vicar of All Saints

The North View of Temple Bruer in the Middle of the Great Heath on the South Side of the City of Lincoln.

Stamford in Lincolnshire, visited Temple Bruer and described a large 'rude and magnificent' monolith standing at the crossroads by the preceptory. He reports that this had been 'Christianised' by carving a Templar cross into the top, a practice often performed on standing stones in northern France, Wales and Cornwall, but very rarely in this area of Britain. Unfortunately, no trace of this stone survives.

In 1726 Samuel Buck made an engraving of what remained of the preceptory. As can be seen from this work, some of the round church remained at that time. Fifty years later, the artist Gough made a similar engraving which shows only the tower, indicating that much of the church had been lost during the intervening years.

In common with many other ruins, the remains of Templar buildings were often damaged or destroyed, or even obliterated—the old stones taken for building material, or moved out of the way of the plough—naturally compromising them as archaeological sites. Few excavations of Templar properties have been carried out at all—but Temple Bruer, uniquely, has been surveyed twice: first in 1841 and then in 1901, each affected by the personality of the surveyor and his attitude towards the Templars.

The Reverend Dr G. Oliver, vicar of the nearby village of Scopwick, undertook the first survey, and confirmed the worst prejudices against the Templars, who for some time had held an evil reputation in these parts—fuelled as elsewhere by the accusation of witchcraft at their trial, and fanned by the ingrained superstition of an age that would seek scapegoats for natural disasters. Oliver reported finding charred bones and bodies encased in walls, evidence of murder and infanticide. He proposed that these remains had belonged to victims of severe Templar law enforcement:

> Some of these vaults were appropriated to uses that it is revolting to allude to. In one of them a niche or cell was discovered, which had been carefully walled up; and within it the skeleton of a man, who appears to have died in a sitting posture, for his head and arms were found hanging between the legs, and the

Above Temple Bruer in 1726, drawn by Samuel Buck, who with his brother Nathaniel set up a business recording old ruins. At this time, part of the round nave was visible as well as the entrance to the crypt.

LINCOLNSHIRE : TEMPLE BRUER

back bowed forward. Immuring [burying alive] was not an uncommon punishment in these places... Another skeleton of an aged man was found in these dungeons, with only one tooth in his head. His body seems to have been thrown down without order or decency, for he lay doubled up; and in the fore part of his skull were two holes, which had evidently been produced by violence. In a corner of one of these vaults, many plain indications of burning exist. The wall stones have assumed the colour of brick, and great quantities of cinders mixed with human skulls and bones; all of which had been submitted to the operation of fire, and some of them perfectly calcined. This horrible cavern had also been closed up with masonry. Underneath the cloisters, between the church and tower, many human bones were discovered, which appear to have been thrown together in the utmost confusion, and lying in different strata, some deep and others very near the surface; amongst which were the skeleton of a very young child, and the skull of an adult, with a round hole in the upper part, into which the end of the little finger might be inserted, and which was probably the cause of death.

W.H. St John Hope carried out the second excavation. This was very different from that of Dr Oliver, who had a taste for the dramatic that sometimes triumphed over his regard for accuracy. He made a number of assumptions based on rumours. St John Hope was more scientific and destined to become one of the leading archaeologists of his time. His method was to carry out a survey using researched information and then decide where to dig trenches.

He begins his report of the operation by referring to Oliver's investigation and proclaims that he has long wanted to ascertain the truth of his findings.

St John Hope's attitude towards the Templars differs markedly from that of Oliver. He considers that the knights were the victims of a sinister conspiracy:

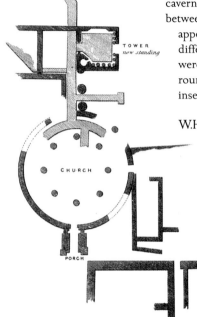

Above The plan of Temple Bruer produced at the time of Reverend Oliver's excavation in 1841. The darker shade indicates remaining structure, the lighter shade underground chambers and tunnels. It was in these he claimed to have found evidence of burial alive and ritual murder.

One is sorely tempted in writing upon matters connected with the Knights Templars to say something about the monstrous persecution and terrible sufferings which the unhappy brethren of the Order endured, during the opening years of the fourteenth century, at the hands of an infamous King of France, a more wicked Pope, and even of a King of England, as an excuse for bringing about their suppression.

As a result, St John Hope's dig refuted much of what Oliver had claimed. Where Oliver found blackened earth and evidence of cremation, St John Hope found:

A large circular oven, about 6 feet in diameter... There can, I think, be little doubt that Dr. Oliver must have opened up part of the reddened stonework, and it is possible that some human remains had fallen or been thrown on to the floor of the oven at the time of some general destruction. But the passage which he shows here as leading to a chamber with an immured skeleton certainly had no existence, for the oven floor was laid upon sloping rock, and outside it to the south the rock comes nearly up to the present surface over quite a considerable area. As Dr. Oliver does not describe his dreadful chamber, but merely says one was found, he was probably putting on record something that had been told him, which his horror of the Templars and all their works caused him to imagine a reality.

It is possible, however, that St John Hope erred a little too much on the side of tolerance. Surviving evidence from Temple Bruer indicates that the brethren were occasionally tempted to break their own rules:

> The Templars were sometimes covetous and extortionate ... a curious instance of which, is recorded in one of the Hundred rolls p. 280, under the date 1270, viz: a complaint of one Adrian Lewin, of Rowston, that Robert de Stratton, then Preceptor of Temple Bruer, had compelled him to supply him with half a mark of silver to enable him to purchase a Roman gold coin, termed a Denarius, that had been found by one Catharine de Foston, and which he ardently longed for.
>
> One of the rules of local Preceptories, however, was that after paying for the cost of their maintenance out of their common fund, they were bound to transmit the surplus annually to the Grand Master of the Temple in London; and they professed to desire that if any Member of their Order died possessed of wealth his money should be buried with him in unconsecrated ground with the imprecation 'Thy money perish with thee'.

The Templars did in fact have specific penalties for proven misdemeanours, including expulsion from the Order for sodomy, desertion or murder. The lesser penalty of losing rank was reserved for such transgressions as losing a slave, fighting with a brother or having sex with a woman. Financial crimes were punished particularly harshly. The Irish Grand Master was suspected of stealing from the order and starved to death in a tiny cell in the London Temple (see page 60). Two embezzlers in Acre were flogged to death. This overt enforcement was seen as necessary in an order that had to maintain the trust of its patrons. No one would deposit money with an organisation that condoned embezzlement.

Above A cross-section of the tower.
Left Grooves in the west wall of the tower are evidence of later building by the Templars as they enlarged the church to include cloisters.

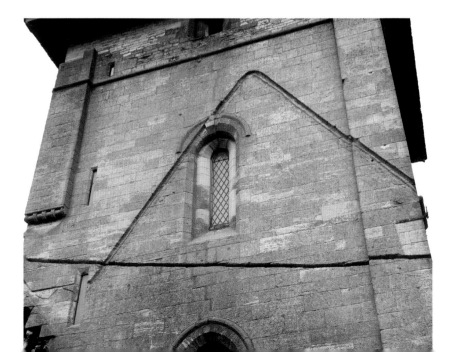

Top The lower half of the door is wider – the romantic suggestion is that it was worn away by knights in armour going to and fro. However, closer inspection reveals that it has been deliberately chiselled rather than worn, for what purpose is unknown.

Above Sections of stone found on the ground floor of the tower. Possibly the remains from one of the eight pillars that supported the rotunda of the round church.

✚ TODAY, WHAT SURVIVES at Temple Bruer is particularly informative as the ruins have been repaired but not altered. The visible structure is the southern tower of the round church. In addition, some of the old Templar manor house has been built into the present fabric of Temple Farm, but sadly this is not open to the public.

Before entering the tower it is worth considering how it would have complemented the church as a whole. The visible tower would have been located at the eastern (altar) end of the building. It would have had a twin a few yards to the north. The two towers would have stood at either side of the altar. The current car-parking area covers the site of the round nave and the main entrance to the church would have been at the western end, which is at the rear.

The north wall, which today holds the main entrance to the tower, would have been an internal wall, and the double piscina cavity to the left of the door would have been placed to the right of the altar. The original ground level was that of the present floor of the tower, and the garden area in front of the tower would have been the floor of the crypt or basement.

On entering the tower, it is necessary to apply a little pressure since the old door is rather stiff. On the ground floor, the area directly to the left of the entrance has been identified as originally containing an altar. It now incorporates fragments of decorative masonry from various sources. There are also fragments of a pillar on the floor. Although it has not been established by archaeological surveys that this pillar was one of the eight built into the round nave, it is similar in size and design to pillars found at churches in Cambridge and Northampton which are considered good examples of Norman round churches.

The Mountain family, who farmed here until recently and owned the preceptory tower, were responsible for preserving the tower and the repairs to the building in the early 1960s. Details of the restoration are displayed on the ground floor.

A single sarcophagus cover lies in the southwest corner. The tomb is that of an unidentified knight or cleric and would have been one of many tombs in the preceptory.

Graffiti above the door indicates the passing of time, and may have been made by a prisoner. Along the west and south sides are arches, between which

IN SEARCH OF THE KNIGHTS TEMPLAR

Right Blind arcading from the ground floor of the west wall. Knights would sit within the alcoves during ceremonies held in this chapel. The last Grand Master of the English Templars, William de la More, was initiated here.

Below The unidentified tomb of a knight or member of the clergy, found on the ground floor.

Below The altar area of the ground floor. In the corner set into the wall is an eight-sectioned piscina. To the left are fragments of masonry collected from the site and sealed into the wall, including the 'cat' (see page 165).

are stone seats. The vaulted ceiling has a single iron ring hanging in the centre, probably as an attachment for lighting.

In the northwest corner a spiral staircase ascends to the first floor. The stairway and the walls of the first floor are covered with graffiti. It is possible to decipher dates carved in the 1600s but many are clearly much older. These probably include so-called masons' marks—either a practical construction guide, or a personal record of an individual mason or carpenter. And it was a common practice in churches throughout the country for pilgrims to incise a record of their visit in the form of a cross.

Some of the inscriptions may have been made by the Templars, who are known to have left graffiti at other sites. Their reason for doing so may vary; like modern 'artists', they may have just wanted to record their visit, to literally leave their mark—or they may have had motives that will never be known.

Some of these marks have been identified as having a more serious function: an attempt to rid the tower of perceived evil. These ritual protection symbols (apotropaic marks) have been used since ancient times by all

cultures, for example the 'eye' drawn on Greek fishermen's boats.

Other significant symbols found in the tower are the 'Triquetra'—the number '3': a sign of the Christian trinity. The letter 'M' is also used, denoting 'Mary'; at Temple Bruer most of the Ms are double, MM perhaps standing for Mary Magdalene, the saint particularly venerated by the Order.

Among the abundant graffiti in Temple Bruer tower, one symbol occurs again and again, far more frequently than any other: the 'Dagaz'. Originally a Scandinavian rune, it symbolised the meeting of two opposed conditions, such as night and day or life and death, implying the triumph of positive good over negative evil.

It is notable that these protection marks seem to follow the Templars around; as well as here at Temple Bruer, they appear in Aslackby, and where they were confined in Lincoln Castle and Clifford's Tower in York. Similar signs are also at Temple Balsall and Rothley Chapel.

This is not to say that the Templars themselves would have left the symbols. It is more likely that they were carved after the suppression of the

Below left The 'Triquetra', symbol of the Holy Trinity, etched into the tower wall in several places.

Below right Apotropaic marks (ritual protection symbols) a common device for spiritual protection, possibly evoking Mary Magdalene, or the Virgin Mary in Majesty.

Bottom left Medieval carving of unknown meaning.

Bottom right The rune 'Dagaz', another apotropaic mark, the most frequent symbol on the tower walls. Inscribed in an attempt to rid the tower of spiritual evil, carried out at an unknown date during the Middle Ages.

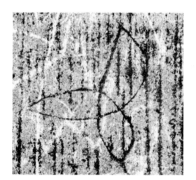

Order by local people, hoping to 'cleanse' the place of the Templars' malevolent legacy. Certainly Temple Bruer retained its evil reputation into the mid-nineteenth century—Dr Oliver's 'finds' would have been no surprise to the more superstitious inhabitants. And, while the later excavation by St John Hope was an altogether more sober affair, one of his conclusions could easily add fuel to the mystical fire: he reasoned that the encased bodies were the remains of a 'pagan' burial—but if this were the case, it raises the question of why the Templars were building on a pagan burial site.

The study of ritual protection symbols is a relatively new field, many having only recently been identified for what they are. Certainly those at Temple Bruer have never been identified as such until now.

Better known is the association of cats with black magic. One of the more ridiculous charges against the Templars at their trial was that they worshipped idols, including a cat. Modern scholarship suggests that the charge of cat worship was probably the consequence of hallucinatory evidence supplied by witnesses under torture. It remains a fact, however, that the carv-

IN SEARCH OF THE KNIGHTS TEMPLAR

ing of a cat can be seen built into the altar area of what is known as 'the Grand Master's Chapel' on the ground floor of the tower. Sylvia Beamon points to the Templars' contact with the East for a possible influence – it is known, for instance, that Ancient Egyptians worshipped the cat, its symbol was the moon.

From the first floor, the narrow spiral stairway, worn by centuries of use, continues to rise but leads nowhere since the upper floor has long since fallen in. This floor would have been the top of the tower, possibly used as a lookout point. It is known that the battlements were crenellated, implying defensive precautions.

Altogether, the tower at Temple Bruer represents one of the few indisputably Templar buildings still standing in Britain.

✝ ASLACKBY

Here on the edge of fen country, the Templars built a preceptory, complete with round church, that was to outlive them by many centuries—though gradually crumbling into ruin or becoming absorbed into other structures, until its existence was all but obliterated except in local legend. Fortunately, written accounts and a rare photographic record can bring it back to life, while the local village church of St James the Great offers more reminders of the Templars' occupation here.

The preceptory was founded in 1164, when Hubert of Rye gave the Templars the church and chapel of Aslackby (pronounced locally as 'Azelby'). Fortuitously, the site was close to a Roman road—always preferred by the Templars, to facilitate transport and communications along the Order's network. The fens stretched eastwards; in the Middle Ages they would have been marshy areas, traversed by boat and raft. (Fenland areas that were dry and habitable still bear the name 'isle', as in Isle of Axholme and Isle of Ely.)

The Templars' preceptory was to the southeast of the main village. Within the preceptory was a round church, the vestiges of which were demolished during the eighteenth century. The 1789 edition of *Camden's Britannia* gives a concise account:

> Here was a round church, now rebuilt as a farmhouse, and still called the Temple. The embattled square tower remains at the south end, of two stories, the upper open to the roof till lately enclosed and fitted up as a chamber by Mr. Douglas, the owner.

The last remnant, a tower much like the one at Temple Bruer (see page 154), stood until 1891 when it fell down on the 'eve of its restoration'. This unlikely coincidence probably had more to do with the ambitions of a local landowner than any act of nature. Prior to its ruin, it was described in John Sander's *Lincolnshire*:

Below A drawing of the ceiling of the ground-floor chamber of the preceptory tower which has unfortunately been lost.

> On the high road from London to Folkingham and Sleaford, and about two miles before you reach Folkingham, you see on the left, lying in the little valley below, the village of Aslackby. And a true specimen of the old English village it is; sloping fields, dotted with sheep, rise around it; a small square embattled tower, hoary with years, seems guarding it on the right, and amid the habitations which repose so calmly around, the church, as conscious of its high and solemn purposes, uprears towards Heaven its simple beauty.
>
> On the left as we enter the village from the high road, we find this tower, which is all that remains of a preceptory of the Knights Templars, built in the reign of Richard the Lion-hearted.
>
> The interior consists of two storeys. The upper one has been roofed and fitted up as a chamber by the occupant of the farmhouse adjoining; the lower one, used as a cellar, appears more in its pristine

state; it is vaulted, with groined arches, having in the centre eight shields bearing various coats of arms, and upon the middle one a cross.

Near to this spot, according to tradition, a round tower formerly stood, which was pulled down, and the materials used to construct the farmhouse above alluded to. This edifice still bears the name that has for centuries been attached to the spot, viz The Temple. On one of the eminences which rise south of the village is said to be the site of the ancient church of the Templars, and it is certain that about ten years ago, a stone coffin of large dimensions was dug up in the adjoining enclosure. There is a tradition among the villagers of a subterraneous passage from this church to the temple before-mentioned.

Note the 'subterraneous passage'—yet another example of the Templars' reputed practice of creating underground facilities. The eight shields mentioned were collected and kept in a garden in Aslackby, until they were moved to a nearby village where they disappeared, apparently sold to a rag and bone man.

In 1312, after the suppression of the Templars, the preceptory was taken into the king's hands, and in 1338 the Hospitallers took over, but did not make it a major commandery. This was probably because the site had lain abandoned and the buildings had become uninhabitable—in this it resembles South Witham (page 150), though without the later benefit of archaeological excavation. The Hospitallers preferred to stay in their own commandaries and use the derelict Templar properties for more basic purposes, such as keeping animals.

Above and right Two rare photographs of the tower at Aslackby taken before 1891, when the tower either fell or was pulled down.

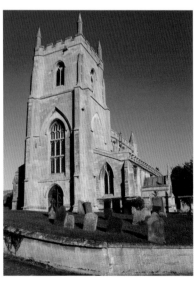

IN SEARCH OF THE KNIGHTS TEMPLAR

✝ TODAY THERE ARE some indications of the Templars' presence in the church of St James the Great in the village. St James, of Compostela in Spain, was a great favourite of crusaders and pilgrims to the Holy Land. His symbol was the scallop shell, and pilgrims would often wear such a badge as a sign of their holy mission. The east window has stained glass depicting three scallops, along with the shields of both Templars and Hospitallers.

On the exterior of the porch is a carving of a 'sundial', said to be used long ago to indicate when services would be held. This theory, though, may not be accurate—several examples of these 'sundials' (as at the Church of the Holy Sepulchre in Northampton) are placed inside the porch, not the best place for the sun, so any other purpose it may have had remains a mystery.

In the porch there is a vast array of carvings and inscriptions in the stone. So detailed are some of the carvings that they seem to be connected, giving the account of a journey by longship. There is no evidence to prove whether or not the Templars had any part in carving this graffiti, though they are well known for leaving their mark in such a way. And the longship in particular may hold a tantalising hint of their maritime adventures.

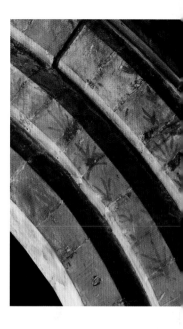

Opposite top The east wall of the porch in St James' Church carries a carving of a longship beneath the sun with waves below. The porch contains a multitude of medieval carvings.
Opposite left The church from the west.
Opposite right The interior looking west.

Above The symbols of the Templars (left), and Hospitallers (right) flank the three scallop shells of St James.
Right Designs similar to this can be found on churches throughout the British Isles. It has been suggested they are sundials for informing locals of service times, but many are located inside the porch away from the sun, so their function remains unclear. It is possible they are sun symbols, remnants of the old religions, similar to those at Royston Cave. Note the numbers actually go in reverse around the circumference – anticlockwise.

Top right A faint wall painting on the central arch.
Left A detail on the church exterior showing a Templar symbol.

✛ ANGEL INN, GRANTHAM

Built by Templars and frequented by kings—the Angel still stands as a monument to hospitality, probably the oldest surviving inn in England. It was originally intended for the traders and pilgrims who thronged the Roman road of Ermine Street, stopping off in this bustling market town. King John, the Templars' particular patron, was only one of several royal guests who had occasion to stay here. Now that the structure has been returned to something resembling its medieval interior, the connection with the Templars is evoked more than ever.

The name 'Angel' was commonly used for medieval hostelries set up by religious establishments. The few that have survived have mostly evolved, appropriately enough, into pubs or inns. The Angel at Grantham is now a hotel, called in modern times the 'Angel & Royal' after those various royal visitors through the ages.

King John stayed in 1213; later it continued its royal patronage when Richard III visited. From what is now called the King's Room, he signed the death warrant for his cousin the Duke of Buckingham (copies are on display in the hotel). Charles I stayed in 1633, ten years before his nemesis Oliver Cromwell.

In 1707 the then landlord Michael Solomon died, and left a legacy of 40 shillings a year to pay for an annual sermon against the 'evils of drunkenness' to be preached on Michaelmas Day—a practice that still continues.

In later life the Angel became an important stop for stagecoaches, carrying passengers and mail, the wide courtyard visible today reflecting the hotel's heyday as a coaching inn. With the coming of the railways, it went into decline.

Lately the inn has undergone a major refurbishment, and much of the interior of the building has been returned to its original condition. By

Right The façade of the recently refurbished Angel and Royal Hotel, said to be the oldest surviving English inn.
Opposite above The angel and crown. In this instance the angel is a symbol of the Templars, founders of the inn; the crown of the many royal visitors through the ages.
Opposite below A carved detail on the hotel's exterior, much worn by erosion, thought to date from the fourteenth century.

IN SEARCH OF THE KNIGHTS TEMPLAR

chance, a medieval fireplace was discovered in the bar. While workmen were removing plaster, they came across a small fireplace. They took it out and revealed a larger one behind it—and one larger still behind that. Finally, after removing the different versions used down the centuries, they arrived at the medieval 9-foot by 6-foot original, still bearing the slots to set up the spit.

As with almost every Templar site, there are legends of tunnels—this time pre-dating most of the building. The cellars at the Angel are thought to go back to the ninth century; running from these cellars are said to be underground passages reaching to the church and market square.

✛ BURTON UPON STATHER

In the church of St Andrew in Burton upon Stather, in a recess in the north wall of the chancel, lies an ancient effigy of a knight—a Templar knight, cast in the cross-legged stance indicating service in the Holy Land. This Templar survived the Crusades and indeed left the Order, married and started a family line that continues to this day: but his final resting place is a memorial to his original vocation.

He was Sir Robert Sheffield, scion of a local family, known to have gone on the Fifth Crusade some time between 1217 and 1221. His effigy is one of several to the family in the church, as a local directory from 1900 describes in terms that are still true today:

> The most ancient being a mutilated figure of a cross-legged knight ... the drapery of this figure is sculptured with great boldness and the details of the armour executed with great precision and the shield bears the arms of Sheffield; supporting a cushion for the head of the knight are remains of angelic figures delicately sculptured; an ancient sword, probably brought from Owston church, is now laid on the figure...

Sir Robert married an heiress, Felicia Tennaby, starting a line of Sheffields whose residence is Sutton Park.

Although family legend implies that Sir Robert was a full knight of the Order, examples of aristocrats who joined as such and then left are very rare, and it may be that he was an associate who fought alongside and supported the Templars. He may have had honorary Templar status, like Richard the Lionheart, or, like William Marshal, was admitted to the Order when he had grown old and death was approaching—an honour bestowed on its most highly regarded supporters.

Opposite Close-up of the effigy of Sir Robert Sheffield, a knight who fought with the Templars. **Right** Sir Robert's effigy now lies in an alcove, to the left of the altar, at the east end of the church.

IN SEARCH OF THE KNIGHTS TEMPLAR

✠ LINCOLN CATHEDRAL

The trial of the Templars in Lincoln took place in the cathedral, one of the very buildings they had helped to bring into being. This first magnificent example of the English Gothic style would most likely not have been possible without the Templars' esoteric knowledge of Muslim architecture, picked up in the Holy Land. Seven centuries later, that Templar connection would be echoed in a modern context, when the chapter house—the actual site of the trial—took the place of Westminster Abbey in the filming of The Da Vinci Code.

The cathedral had been started shortly after the Conquest, in 1072, with typically massive Norman walls and arches. Most of the present structure dates from the first part of the thirteenth century, when the cathedral was rebuilt in an innovative style now called Early English Gothic. Essentially, this fusion of simplicity and elegance allowed space and light. The Templars had certainly learnt in the East the techniques of building a huge structure that was supported externally and could contain large delicate windows and vast open spaces, the Arabs having inherited the ancient Greek texts relating to geometry, such as the work of Euclid. Lincoln Cathedral was the first building to be higher than the pyramids.

This form of building was revolutionary in medieval Europe and, even now, the methods of construction remain a mystery, subject to a kind of 'backwards engineering', where experts have examined the buildings and made well-informed guesses about how they were constructed. This tradition of esoteric architectural knowledge among the Templars has been seized upon by Masonic historians to give a possible genesis for their own traditions, which borrow symbolically from the stone mason's craft.

Some historians point to the Templars as the conduit not only for the specialist architectural knowledge required for this and other Gothic

Right Looking east, towards the cathedral from the castle.
Opposite above Lincoln Cathedral interior, looking east.
Opposite below Detail of Romanesque carving, on the left-hand arch of the west front. The Romanesque style was employed by the early Normans and often used symbols that appear overtly pagan and licentious.

IN SEARCH OF THE KNIGHTS TEMPLAR

cathedrals that were constructed throughout western Europe, but also for the finance—a natural connection, given their international standing as bankers.

Whatever the extent of their involvement with the cathedral, it was here, in the chapter house, that they were tried in March and April 1310, each brother being asked a series of questions. The process was excruciatingly prolonged but, for all the attention to detail, no evidence was found to support the charges against the Order. The lack of any progress prompted the inquisitors to examine all the English Templars together and in March 1311 the Templars held in Lincoln Castle were transferred to London. Despite further hardships and more interrogation, still no evidence was found against the brethren, and less than a year later they were released. Some of the Lincolnshire brothers were allowed to return home to live out their days at the abandoned preceptory of Temple Bruer.

TEMPLI MILITES IN DOMO CAPITVLARI IVDICATI MCCCX

Above A stained-glass window recording the examination of the Templars which occurred in the chapter house in 1310. The prolonged inquisition lasted two years, with the Templars eventually being released due to lack of evidence. This window dates from the Victorian period.
Left The chapter house exterior.

✝ THE MAIN ENTRANCE to the cathedral is through the west door; the chapter house is situated to the north of the cathedral, accessed through the cloisters.

The Templars' trial is commemorated in the chapter house by Victorian stained glass.

In August 2005, when Dan Brown's book *The Da Vinci Code* was being filmed in the chapter house, artists were commissioned to produce panels that would sit within each alcove of the arcading, to give the impression of wall paintings. The artists then discovered for themselves a feature of the structure that had long puzzled historians and architects: the alcoves, which might reasonably be expected to be uniform, in fact vary enormously in size.

This variation is surprising: it seems that the masons who were unable to get anything near a uniform size in a 6-foot space were in the process of constructing a cathedral 525 feet high—the world's tallest building until the spire collapsed in 1625.

Nobody can conclusively account for the variation, which occurs throughout the cathedral—and in others too. Some say the builders were simply being rushed and unsure of what they were doing, while others suggest that all the idiosyncrasies were intentional and contain a code of their own.

Above Two interior views of the chapter house.
Left Authentic-looking wall paintings, re-created for the filming of *The Da Vinci Code*, where Lincoln Cathedral chapter house stood in for the chapter house at Westminster Abbey.

✠ LINCOLN CASTLE

Within a tower of this ancient fortress, members of the Order of the Knights Templar were imprisoned for two years, awaiting trial. Accused of heresy among other grave sins, they would in due course plead their innocence in the nearby cathedral. Meanwhile, they expressed their faith in a way that would have given focus to their daily devotions: carving a series of religious images on the stone walls of their prison. These carvings are not only an enduring symbol of their belief, but a poignant testament to the last days of the Order.

Below The western hill or motte at Lincoln Castle, originally a prehistoric structure. It is one of the two hills on which William the Conqueror built his castle. In later life it became the burial ground for the prison, receiving the bodies of executed prisoners.

Lincoln Castle has acquired a reputation among mediums and psychics as one of the most spiritually oppressive locations in the country, with numerous reports of ghosts and paranormal disturbances—from dogs that refuse to enter the gates to spectres that attempt to abduct children. Whatever sceptics may have to say, certainly the castle has witnessed long centuries of suffering and death, which have sparked legends of 'atmosphere' and unquiet spirits.

The Romans had built a castle here, and the Norman invaders followed their example, first with a wooden stockade and then a stone fortress. By the time of the Templars' arrest in 1307, this had become a substantial structure with a massive perimeter wall punctuated at various points by towers.

One of these, the Cobb Tower, had been built in the thirteenth century, and was where the Templars were held. 'Cobb' means 'round'—the name may derive from the shape of the tower, or perhaps from a recent discovery under the tower of round chiselled blocks of stone called cobbs. These were shaped to be used in a giant catapult sited on top of the tower, a Norman means of defence that would have ranged over the streets approaching the castle from the northeast.

The catapult was gone by the early nineteenth century, when the tower

was first used for public executions. The local population would gather in the streets below and at the appointed time the prisoner would be led from their cell in the tower up the steps to the scaffold. The occasion was used as an excuse for a market, fair and general party. The graves of the executed prisoners remain on the hill at the south of the castle — another haunted location.

The Templars had been brought to the tower from their estates throughout Lincolnshire and the surrounding counties, and here they would be held until 1310, and their trial in the cathedral.

Above The prisoners' graveyard, which is thought to be haunted.
Above right The *oriel* window (meaning a window that projects from the house) situated by the East Gate. It was originally a feature of John of Gaunt's house in Lincoln, before being transferred to the castle in 1850.
Right Looking east past the observatory tower to the cathedral.

Above Interior of the Cobb Tower, where Templars were imprisoned while awaiting trial. Many have supposed that the Templars were chained but, initially at least, they were allowed to walk around quite freely.

Far left Cobb Tower from outside the castle; the view is similar to what would have been seen by a crowd gathered to watch a public execution. The scaffold would have been on top of the tower.

Left Cobb Tower from inside the castle.

✝ COBB TOWER IS SITED at the northeast point of the castle, to the right of the main entrance. The carvings are easy to locate as they have recently been protected by Perspex.

The only other comparable carvings made by the Templars while in prison are those at Chinon Castle in France. Other Templar carvings have been found in the Holy Land, and also in Europe, for example in Royston Cave (see page 96).

Below Crucifixion scene, found by the window.
Bottom left St Christopher, a popular medieval saint, with Jesus on his right shoulder.
Bottom right Carvings found to the left on entering the tower. This figure bears a resemblance to a figure found in Royston Cave.
Right and far right Two crosses, in a similar style to the crosses found on Templar tomb lids and other Templar carvings in Chinon Castle.

YORKSHIRE

YORKSHIRE PROVIDED the Templars with some of their largest and most productive estates. Such was the extent of their holdings that they ran what was almost a mini-state in the county, with an overall head of preceptories who was equal to the Grand Masters of Ireland, Scotland and Wales. ✚ Other monastic houses existed here before the Templars, primarily the Order most closely associated with them, the Cistercians. These 'monks of the frontier' laid the groundwork of enterprise that the Templars would later build on: to maximise profits by mass production and economies of scale. In Yorkshire the most valuable product was wool, and the Cistercians had been one of the first to selectively breed sheep, creating a variety that surpassed all others in quality and quantity of wool. ✚ The Templars made their mark in towns as well as the countryside — literally so in the case of the iron crosses they used to identify their properties. These crosses, some of which still survive in museums, denoted the Order's exemption from local taxes, a privilege known to have caused resentment. ✚ One of the largest Templar enterprises in the county was the port of Faxfleet on the Humber, which also had a full preceptory. Nothing now remains of it, and the preceptories of Copmanthorpe, Foulbridge, Temple Cowton, Temple Newsam and Whitley have similarly been obliterated. There are still remains to be seen at Penhill, with its solitary ruined chapel; Ribston, with its surviving chapel built on to a manor house; Temple Hirst, with an original tower; and Westerdale, where a Victorian church houses grave slabs and a boundary marker, poignant remnants of the Order's former presence. ✚ After their arrests in the county the Templars were held at York Castle, in what was later called Clifford's Tower. They left no discernible trace of their presence here, before they were transferred to the Tower of London and released soon afterwards. ✛

✛ PENHILL

(WENSLEYDALE) *High on the Yorkshire moors, the Templars built a preceptory that took its name from the isolated peak on whose side it stood. Fallen into ruin long ago, only the undulating ground in a field suggests its buried remains, although the chapel has left a visible footprint to this day. Stone crosses are a reminder of the old estate's boundaries, but curious stone 'coffins' on the site are not so easily explained away. No such mystery lingers in how the Templars would have used the land itself—as well as the usual sheep-rearing and farming, the wide open spaces made it ideal horse country.*

Being primarily cavalry fighters, all medieval knights, secular and religious, needed a steady supply of horses to replace those killed or injured in battle. For the Templars, this meant breeding the type of stocky charger they favoured, one that would have the requisite qualities of stamina, temperament, speed and agility—there was no place on the battlefield for highly strung thoroughbreds. After training, these horses would be shipped to the Holy Land in the Templars' own vessels, from stud farms in both England and Ireland. Penhill sent its horses via the east coast ports, the largest of which was Faxfleet on the Humber.

Not that the Templars would have concentrated their energies on just this one enterprise: as ever, they worked with the land to make the best possible profit from whatever was available. As well as horses at the Penhill estate, they would have had flocks of the ubiquitous sheep, and other domestic animals.

Perhaps there is some link with sheep in the Templars' dedication of the chapel to St Catherine (or Katherine) of Alexandria, patron saint of spinners and weavers among many other causes. She was certainly a favourite of the Order; Temple Church in both Cornwall and Bristol were also dedicated to her, and she appears in the carvings of Royston Cave.

The land and timber for the preceptory had been granted in 1170 by Roger de Mowbray, a keen supporter of the Templars who was later to have the rare—possibly unique—distinction of being ransomed by the Order. In the course of a highly eventful life, Roger fought in several Crusades, the last time at the age of sixty-five, when he was one of the few Christians to survive the decisive Battle of Hattin and be held in captivity. This is when the Templars,

Previous page Looking from the Templars' place of confinement, Clifford's Tower, to the site of their trial in Yorkshire, the Minster. **Below** The view across Wensleydale from Penhill Tor.

IN SEARCH OF THE KNIGHTS TEMPLAR

notwithstanding their own rejection of ransom, recognised the value of Roger's support and bought his freedom. He died shortly after and was apparently buried in the Holy Land —though, interestingly, at Bylands Abbey in Yorkshire there is a grave known as the 'tomb of Roger de Mowbray'.

De Mowbray is a good example of one of the Templars' more generous benefactors. From 1150 to 1186 his donations, as recorded by Evelyn Lord, included not only the land and timber for Penhill itself (and two other houses), but also:

Brimham, North Yorkshire, half a carucate [equal to 60 acres of land]
Hampton in Arden, Warwickshire, advowson [right to appoint priests] of the church
Balsall, Warwickshire, tenements
Bagby, Yorkshire, arable and pasture
Thorpe, Yorkshire, 2 bovates [equal to 15 acres of land]
Weedley, Yorkshire, demesne [property retained by the church] and carucate [equal to 120 acres of land]
Althorpe and Burnham, Lincolnshire, rents and the advowson of the church and chapel
Beltoft, Lincolnshire, services of tenants
Keadby, Lincolnshire, all land and wood

Above A Templar's tomb, which was probably brought into the chapel area from the surrounding fields.

When the Order was suppressed in 1308, Penhill preceptory, like all other Templar properties, was handed over to the Hospitallers—who, however, seemed in no hurry to develop the site. Its buildings soon fell into ruin. The preceptory itself was eventually obliterated, the process hastened no doubt by local people removing and reusing the stones, and the site has never been excavated. What remained of the chapel was investigated in 1840, as *A History of the County of York* records:

There was a chapel at Penhill, of which the ruins, containing an altar and some stone coffins, were excavated some years since. This no doubt adjoined the cemetery just mentioned, as a number of coffins were found outside the east wall. Early grants are recorded for the support of the lights of St Katherine and the Holy Cross at Penhill, and the chapel is mentioned at the time of the suppression of the Order as containing a chalice worth 20s, and a few books and vestments.

(These 'lights' were candles kept burning in honour of the patron.)

Top left A Templar marker which denotes the extent of the Templar land and the tithe-free status they enjoyed.

Top right The Knights Hospitaller chapel at Brimpton, Berkshire. Penhill chapel would have been a similar size and design.

Above left As with most Templar sites in the British countryside a 'Temple Farm' continues to cultivate the lands the Order once held.

Above right Consistent with Templar symbolism, an eight-sectioned piscina that would have stood to the right of the altar.

Opposite above left One of the two mysterious graves, about three feet long – they have no known purpose. They are situated in front of the altar to the left and right.

Opposite above right Between the two small graves is a post hole, perhaps to support the rood screen, dividing the clergy from the congregation.

Opposite bottom Looking across the chapel from the northeast, the altar area is marked by a stone rectangle to the left.

✚ THE EXTENT of the preceptory estate continues to be defined by markers bearing the Templar cross pattée, which are found in the fields and built into the drystone walls. Some are probably copies, but others may be original.

The old preceptory lies on a scenic ridge reached by a steep tree-lined path, hazardous in wet weather. The chapel ruins, fenced off from wandering sheep, are approached from the western end. The original entrance is in the south wall; to the right of this is a lidless Templar tomb, probably recovered from outside the chapel. Beyond this tomb is a single post hole.

At either side of the posthole, overgrown and hidden, are two small stone cavities which resemble tombs in the ground with displaced lids. These are described as 'graves' in the site information, and also in excavation reports, but it seems unlikely that they would have been used for orthodox burials. The two 'graves' are the right size to accommodate a sword, but this would raise the question of why weapons would be kept buried beside the altar.

Beyond the two 'coffins' are the foundations of the altar and rood screen; the screen divided the church, keeping the most sacred area around the altar isolated for the clergy. At the South Witham excavation (page 150) a chapel similar in size to the one here was found, along with fragments of stained glass and lead. Both chapels were comparable to the small Hospitaller chapel in Brimpton, Berkshire, which is still standing.

✚ RIBSTON

(NORTH YORKSHIRE) *The Templars built their preceptory at Ribston, in the valley of the River Nidd, on land donated by Sir Robert de Ros, one of their most illustrious supporters. The son-in-law of the Scottish king, he had been one of the barons appointed to enforce the terms of Magna Carta in 1215. Robert had the honour of being buried in London's Temple Church, where a well-preserved effigy remains with the de Ros coat of arms — though whether this is Robert or another member of the family is unclear. All that has been preserved of the Templars' tenure at Ribston is their rectangular chapel of St Andrew, now attached to Ribston Hall, the stately home later built on the site.*

The chapel is on private land and in private ownership, not usually open to the public — access to the interior was granted for the purpose of this book. But the exterior can be viewed from a distance, by taking the footpath that runs through the estate, which roughly follows the boundaries of the old preceptory.

The last preceptor of Ribston was William de Grafton, whose later history throws up a puzzle. After the suppression and arrest in 1308, he, like the other Templars, was later released and, as part of his penance, he went to Selby Abbey in North Yorkshire. In 1331 he successfully applied to be released from his monastic vows, as a contemporary document states (in the translation by Dennis Garner):

> The Master of the Temple with the assent of his brethren absolves from his vow William de Grafton one of the brethren of the Order and granted that having laid aside the habit of the Temple he may be allowed to turn himself to the secular state which King Edward II and the present King have confirmed.

This is more than twenty years after the Order was officially suppressed, but apparently there is still a 'Master of the Temple' to give his permission, and William is still 'one of the brethren'.

Above Two Templar crosses built into the fabric of the east and south walls.
Right In Temple Church in London the effigy of a de Ros, popularly attributed to Robert de Ros, the man who originally donated the land on which the Templars built the preceptory at Ribston.

IN SEARCH OF THE KNIGHTS TEMPLAR

Ribston had provided another surprise at the time of the audit following the suppression. The *History of the County of York* records that it 'was remarkable as possessing two silver cups, three masers, and ten silver spoons—more secular plate than all the other Yorkshire preceptories put together.' There is no obvious reason for this affluence.

After the suppression, Ribston was held by the king until 1324, when the Hospitallers managed to take possession as decreed by the pope—this was a typical delay. The buildings remained standing until the late 1600s, by which time the Goodricke family had been resident for nearly two hundred years. As Charles Alfred Goodricke, in his *Incidents in the lives of some of the Goodrickes of Yorkshire* from 1490 to 1833, states:

> The rebuilding of the residence at Ribston appears now to have occupied Sir Henry's attention, and he took it in hand... Sir Henry evidently considered the old buildings of the Knights Templars, which had been converted into a residence more than a hundred years previously, were worn out and no longer suited to either the time or circumstances. He accordingly pulled the whole of them down, excepting a very small portion of the chapel, in 1673 and upon the same site, he constructed the new Hall, the main portion of which we see at the present time.

Interestingly, there is a Templar element in All Saints' Church at nearby Spofforth. Two Templar crosses are 'hidden' in its outer walls, one high up above the north aisle roof, the other near ground level at the east end. These are of a different sort of stone to the rest of the church. In common with practices found elsewhere, they are likely to have been rescued from the old preceptory buildings as a powerful spiritual token of the Templars.

Above Three carved heads from the south wall of the chapel.
Left The chapel is attached to the south wing of the later Ribston Hall.

Above A rare Templar marker stone, sited in the grounds of Ribston Hall.

Above right The interior of the chapel looking east.

Right middle Either side of the altar at St Andrew's are graves said to belong to Templars.

Bottom left The three Bougets (water bags) that form the coat of arms of the de Ros family.

Bottom right On the ceiling of Ribston Chapel are painted various shields related to the Templars. This is the shield of the last English Grand Master, William de la More.

Left, far left and below
Nineteenth-century stained glass in the western window of Ribston. (Left) The seal of the Templars. (Far left) The Lamb of God, *Agnus Dei*, sign of St John the Baptist. (Below) A Templar knight (left) and a Hospitaller knight (right) flank St Andrew, the patron saint of the chapel.

✛ TEMPLE HIRST

(SOUTH YORKSHIRE) *The second Templar preceptory to be built in Yorkshire, Temple Hirst was the core of one of the greatest wool-producing estates in the country. Strategically sited on the River Aire, it could export its valuable cargo to Europe via the port of Faxfleet on the east coast, building up considerable wealth for the Order. All that remains now of that centre of energy and industry is a single tower, attached to a later manor house, and an account of the Templars' trial in which the brothers here were charged with one of the more unlikely offences.*

Land for the preceptory was first donated in 1152 by Ralph, brother of the Templar Grand Master Richard de Hastings. Other than their participation in the wool trade, little is known of the Templars' activities during the lifetime of the preceptory. After the Order was suppressed in 1308, there was some record of their possessions, according to *A History of the County of York*:

> We have an account of the furniture of the chapel, which included two chalices, one silver and one gilt, a cross, a pyx, a censer, some half-a-dozen service books and a few vestments [and] some 200 acres of land, and the preceptory itself ... consisting of a hall, chapel, kitchen, larder, and outbuildings.

At their trial in London, the Templars were accused of an incredible spectrum of offences, from worshipping heads, cats and goats to spitting and defecating on the cross, sodomy and witchcraft. The Temple Hirst brothers were specifically charged with worshipping a calf. When a charge was so outlandish, and without independent corroboration, the net effect was often to stress the innocence of the Order.

Below Temple Hirst Hall from the south.

IN SEARCH OF THE KNIGHTS TEMPLAR

Above The original Norman arch, the Templars' entrance to the hall.
Left The brick tower at the east end of the hall, thought to be one of an orginal pair. The location of its lost twin is unknown.

✠ THE TOWER is believed to be one of a pair; the location of the other is unknown. The only other remaining feature from the Templars' time is the south porch, a fine Norman arch with plain capitals. It may be that the tower and arch were part of a Templar chapel—the building is appropriately orientated (see Appendix, page 242). The manor house built on to the original Norman tower was once a farmhouse and now serves as a retirement home, so the site is on private land and can be viewed only from the road.

✚ WESTERDALE

(NORTH YORKSHIRE) *Nothing is left of the Westerdale preceptory itself, and an early Victorian church stands on the site of the original Templar chapel. But in the porch of this church are evocative monuments to the Order: grave slabs showing the evolution of design, linking them with both European and Scottish tradition; and a boundary marker, a reminder of the Templars' once great estates. A nearby Norman bridge now goes nowhere, but its stones may well have been worn smooth by Templar men—one of whom, the last preceptor himself, was once caught openly advertising blasphemy.*

Westerdale, high on the north Yorkshire moors, was donated to the Templars by Guy de Bonaincurt, a gift confirmed by King John in 1203. Very little else is known about the activities of the Templars here.

Dennis Garner has drawn attention to a curious story related in the records of the trial of the Templars in England, concerning the Sheriff of York's testimony against William de la Fenne, the last preceptor of Westerdale.

> The Sheriff said that before the arrests, Brother William was invited to dine with him and his wife. He showed them a book and gave it to the Sheriff's wife to read. In it she found a slip mentioning that Jesus wasn't the Son of God and that he wasn't born of a virgin, although he was the son of Mary and Joseph. It also said that Jesus was a false prophet and that he was crucified for his own sins and not to save the human race. The Sheriff's wife showed the book to her husband who spoke to William de la Fenne and asked him about the slip. The Preceptor of Westerdale said that it had been written by Magnus Ribaldus (the Great Joker). After that William took the book home with him.
>
> During the trial, William de la Fenne confirmed the Sheriff's testimony but he said that he didn't know what the book or the slip contained because he didn't read Latin.

Opposite top left
Christ Church, Westerdale.
Opposite top centre
The ancient bridge that leads nowhere.
Below In the valley to the north of the village stands a bridge, repaired in times past, its stones well worn by traffic. The bridge is now abandoned, but thought to have been originally built at the time of the Templars.

This story is unique, and apparently true, but raises all kinds of questions. Why would a Christian monk, a preceptor at that, carry around heretical material he professed not to understand, and then start passing it around in company? And if he did understand it, and endorsed it, he would have believed Jesus was a false prophet—so who was the prophet William regarded as true?

It seems some of the Templars at least were capable of adding to the fog of rumour and suspicion that enveloped them.

✠ THE CHURCH housing the Templar grave slabs and boundary marker is to the west of the main village street. The Reverend George Young summed up the function of boundary markers in 1817, in his history of Whitby (on the coast and not far from Westerdale) and Streonshalch Abbey: 'Many stone crosses and markers were set up to prevent disputes over territory and to serve as land markers ... this plan was especially adopted by the knights Templars and Hospitallers.'

The stones here show consistency of design with each other, and examples of Templar stone markers and graves found elsewhere.

The ancient bridge in Westerdale now goes into a field. The writer and Templar expert Tim Staniland feels it is related to the Templars' tenure as it was obviously of considerable importance in times past, judging by the well-worn stones.

Crosses clockwise from top right The top of a marker cross, roughly hewn; Romanesque carved grave slab; A rough-hewn slab, possibly a grave slab. Part of a broken cross rests on top; Base of stepped cross grave slab, showing an eight-petalled floral design, and the lower part of a sword or dagger. Two incisions at either side are unclear; A grave slab similar to Templar graves at Tomar and Kilmory, showing a dagger and a bow and arrow.

✠ CLIFFORD'S TOWER

(YORK) *Within the thick stone walls of this massive tower, the site of atrocities in centuries past, twenty-five members of the Knights Templar were held prisoner. They were confined for several years, from late 1307, awaiting trial on the charges of heresy and witchcraft made against the entire Order. In other places of imprisonment, the brothers made their mark—literally, carving symbols and graffiti on the walls. Nothing like this has yet been found in the tower, though evidently someone thought it necessary to carve protective runes in their wake.*

Clifford's Tower was not known by that name at the time of the Templars' imprisonment. It was not until 1322 that Roger de Clifford, having supported a failed uprising against Edward II, was executed and his body hung in chains from the walls of the tower that would bear his name thereafter.

The mound on which Clifford's Tower stands, above a prehistoric burial site, is the original motte of William the Conqueror's first castle here, built of wood in 1068. Having suppressed the north of England so ruthlessly, William needed to set up strong defences as soon as possible. Like Lincoln Castle, York was built to pre-empt any uprisings or the anticipated invasions from Scandinavia on behalf of the land's previous masters, the Vikings.

Over a hundred years later, a tower on the site now occupied by Clifford's Tower saw one of England's most infamous atrocities. During a wave of anti-Semitism, a spate of massacres took place against the Jews. On the night of 16 March 1190, Jewish families fleeing from a mob sought refuge in the wooden tower. Despite the presence of children, the mob set fire to it. When the Jews realised what was happening, many chose to take their own lives. Of the others, those not burned alive were killed by the mob. Ultimately none survived. Tragically, one of the reasons Jews chose to live in cities such as York and Lincoln was the belief that they would receive protection in the

Above Clifford's Tower, site of many bloody events, stands on a prehistoric mound, possibly a burial chamber.
Right Clifford's Tower from the castle museum.

IN SEARCH OF THE KNIGHTS TEMPLAR

royal castles from the kings they had supported.

The tower was rebuilt in stone and it was here that the Yorkshire Templars were held before and during their provincial trial, which took place within the chapter house at York Minster.

While no identifiable trace of the Templars' presence in the tower has been found—and just where they were held is not known—this could be simply because parts of the walls are inaccessible, the middle floor having been lost. Like Lincoln Castle, and other prisons in which the Templars were held, Clifford's Tower may contain carvings and graffiti made by the knights. A Dagaz rune (see page 163) has been found, but this almost certainly post-dates the Templars, and would have been made to rid the tower of its 'evil spirits'.

Above left The interior of the tower. The wooden floors have been lost, making access to where the Templars may have been held difficult. There is access to the top of the tower with commanding views over the city of York.

Above Interior of the small chapel sited within the tower. The decorative stone work of the chapel probably came from another building. Ironically this may have been a Templar chapel thought to have stood close by.

Left Dagaz rune, a ritual protection mark etched into the southeast stairwall.

WALES AND THE BORDERS

THIS WAS THE KIND OF TERRITORY to bring out the warrior more than the monk: in common with Scotland and Ireland, Wales with its independent tribal kingdoms did not accede easily to the Norman Conquest. While rebellion erupted within the Celtic stronghold, the border lands were even more tempestuous, the Marcher lords who ruled there having a high degree of independence from the English Crown in return for services rendered — services that usually were of benefit to Marcher lords. ✚ But it was Hospitaller country rather than Templar, perhaps because the Templars were thought by both Welsh and Marcher lords to be too close to the hated English. Certainly it was no accident that the most profitable Templar estates were in the most pacified areas of Norman Britain. ✚ The Templars had a few scattered properties in Wales itself, of which only Llanmadoc church on the Gower peninsula survives. Their nearest preceptories were north–south along the border; of these, only Garway in Herefordshire has any remains to be seen. In any case, it seems that few knights would actually be resident in Welsh properties, and none of them was recorded during the trial as originating from Wales. ✚ Given its commercial imperatives, the Order probably tried to generate some profit where it could. Appraising the profitability of donated land, they would sometimes choose to reduce the area they farmed directly, leasing out some acres to be managed by others. ✚ Two individual sites shed light on the Templars in very different ways: the tomb of St Thomas de Cantilupe in Hereford Cathedral, and the round chapel in Ludlow Castle. ✚ After the Templars' suppression, many brothers (who had been warned in advance of the arrests) could use the land to their final advantage, as they did in Ireland and Scotland — moving out of the reach of the king's men and seeking shelter in the valleys and hills. ✤

✛ GARWAY

(HEREFORDSHIRE) *St Michael's Church is rather like the pragmatic Templars themselves: dedicated to a holy cause that espouses peace, but equipped to cope with war. Sited in the border lands between Wales and England, then a region of perennial conflict, it is dwarfed by its massive defensive tower—a marked contrast to the church itself, which is exquisitely beautiful. It is one of the Templars' most enigmatic properties too: a Christian church, but bearing in its very fabric subtle signs of an older, wilder religion that once held sway—esoteric carvings and fantastical images of heathen gods and nature spirits.*

Previous page Interior of the Garway dovecote – some of the 666 nesting holes.
Opposite top left St Michael's from the north.
Opposite top right The dovecote was probably rebuilt in the fourteenth century by Hospitallers.
Below Looking across to St Michael's Church from the west, the top of the round dovecote can just be seen slightly to the right of centre.

Whatever their significance to Templars, the pagan images in St Michael's come from a tradition of Romanesque carving that originated in this area, called, appropriately, the Herefordshire School. This arose after the Norman Conquest, with influence from mainland Europe, and features such elements as writhing foliage, strange beasts, and people in various guises, carved with great skill and imagination.

The tradition has a mixture of influences, seeming to be the bridge between pagan nature worship and Christianity. The early Christian Church did not seek to obliterate all aspects of pre-existing faiths; rather, it subsumed them. So green men, corn dollies, harvest festival, spring festival (Easter) among others all metamorphosed into aspects of the Christian faith and ritual.

St Michael's is far from the only example—local churches abound with such icons as the archetypal fertility symbol, the green man (of which St Michael's has a good example), and the explicit symbol of female sexuality, the sheela na gig. The church of Kilpeck two miles away has a particularly rich collection of Herefordshire-style carvings. Many of the images resemble Scandinavian carvings, recalling the Norse origins of the Normans.

Long before the Normans arrived, Garway was a sacred site. In the sixth century, a gift of 108 acres of land was made by Guorfoddw, the king of

IN SEARCH OF THE KNIGHTS TEMPLAR

Archenfield (the ancient name for the southwest corner of Hereford), on which to build a church. The choice of land may have been influenced by the holy well at what is now the southeast of the churchyard. It was about this time that Christianity was gaining strength in England as a whole — though much of Wales had been Christian for centuries already.

The Templars founded their preceptory in 1185–88; it represented the most important house in the area, its administration reaching as far down as Swansea. As a sign of its distinction, it was visited by Jacques de Molay in 1294 in his then role as Grand Master of England. (He was later head of the Order, and was to be burnt to death by command of the French king.)

The present church was built over the Templars' first, one of their typical 'round' churches; its foundations are still visible on the north side beneath the enigmatic carvings and symbols in the church structure, augmented by graffiti and esoteric inscriptions, both inside and out.

To the south of the church lies a dovecote, typical of the medieval style but massive by today's standards. Oddly, it has 666 holes — quite why the Number of the Beast was thought appropriate is a matter of conjecture. Inside there would have been a rotating wooden ladder, a 'potence', that gave access to all the nests. Despite any sinister connotation, it is one of the finest Norman examples in the country, and is now on private land. An inscription over the entrance says that it was built by Brother Richard in 1326, by which time the Templars were gone. But at the time of their suppression, records dating from 1313 show a 'broken' dovecote. So Brother Richard probably rebuilt it.

The dove may be a Christian symbol of peace, but it also served a very practical purpose for the Templars and their household. The birds and their eggs were a good all-year-round source of food. They bred well and the youngsters were a particular delicacy. Even their dung was a rich fertiliser. A well-stocked dovecote would be especially valuable in a castle under siege.

Below and bottom
Examples of the Herefordshire school of Romanesque carving from the nearby Kilpeck church: a 'sheela na gig', a female fertility figure (below), and a 'green man' (bottom). These show stylistic similarities to those found at St Michael's in Garway.

✠ THE MOST DOMINANT FEATURE of the building—its massive tower, attached to the church by a short corridor—reflects the time and place in which it was built. Even in an age when warfare was commonplace, the border lands between Wales and England were exceptionally turbulent. As the chief Celtic power in the west, the Welsh resisted a range of hostile forces from pagan Anglo-Saxons to Christian Normans, while the Marcher lords—rulers along the border—were out for themselves and no other. Such towers would provide shelter for local people in times of attack.

St Michael's tower may also have been used as a prison at some point, though whether by the Templars or the Hospitallers who inherited the site—or later still—is unclear.

The tower may have originally been detached from the main building. A couple of hundred years after the Templars left, the tower's height was increased by about 8 feet; it is now 70 feet high. The connecting passage is around 400 years old and was built with reused material, as evidenced by the Templar tomb lid providing a lintel above the east window.

Moving clockwise around the exterior of the church from the tower, the foundations of the old round church can be seen. These were uncovered when the site was excavated in 1927, by a Mr Jack. This round church would be one of eight known round naves built by the Order. Those at Bristol, Aslackby, Temple Bruer, Hereford and Holborn (London), are no longer visible; the London Temple still stands, while at Dover the remains of the foundations can still be seen.

The Garway site gives a good picture of the original round church, the width of the foundations conveying the strength and size of the building.

Above these foundations is a plaque: 'Foundations of a round church of the Knights Templar 12th century, exposed 1927'. And above the plaque, quite

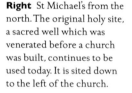

Right St Michael's from the north. The original holy site, a sacred well which was venerated before a church was built, continues to be used today. It is sited down to the left of the church.

IN SEARCH OF THE KNIGHTS TEMPLAR

high up, is a carving of the *Dextra Dei*, or Hand of God, emerging from the clouds.

On the existing north wall can be seen the blocked-up door and window, dating from the thirteenth century.

On the east wall of the church, there is a series of crosses. First, a patriarchal cross with crosslets—a general Christian motif; then further along, on the chapel wall, a little lower than eye level, a Maltese cross—the particular sign of the Knights Hospitaller—is carved into the brickwork. Also here is a cross fourchée ('forked'). This design reflects Christian piety and was popular as a decorative cross in medieval heraldry. The design ties into an age-old trust in the pagan magic of the forked stick.

Above this at each end of the window arch are carved heads, showing perhaps a grand master or a bishop wearing a mitre and alongside a death-like head.

Moving to the south wall, a number of carved symbols can be seen: two symmetrical Jerusalem crosses, one a cross potent; a swastika (an ancient

Above, clockwise from top left The Hand of God, *Dextra Dei*; The figure of 'death' on the east wall window; An unknown cleric found on the east wall window; Patriarchal cross with crosslets; A forked cross or 'cross fourchée'; Below the north wall, the massive foundations of the original round church.
Centre The cross of the Hospitallers, now known as the 'Maltese cross'.

Top left A swastika, one of the oldest symbols known to man. Here rotating clockwise, a spinning wheel with cosmic symbolism.
Top middle Cross with crosslets, another crusader symbol.
Top right The 'cross potent', used during the Crusades as the cross of Jerusalem, usually with smaller crosslets.

Above left Located on the west wall of the Templar chapel, the *Agnus Dei*, the Lamb of God, symbol of St John the Baptist found at a number of Templar sites.
Right middle The winged dragon, the gryphon, with its forked tongue. Associated with flying serpents, and related to other serpent symbols found at the church of St Michael.
Above right 'TK' sign and '8' or hourglass. A further example of the importance of the number 8 to the Templars.

symbol of peace before being twisted by the Nazis); a T with a K carved into it; and the figure '8' (or hourglass symbol), commonly used by Templars, as at Santa Maria Do Olival in Tomar, Portugal.

Near the west door of the chapel there is a Lamb of God (*Agnus Dei*) high up on the wall—a motif used by both Templar and Hospitaller orders.

Above the main door is a window and above that a winged dragon or griffin, a common feature in medieval manuscripts and decoration.

An ancient door with an engraved iron handle leads into the church.

On the left is a font with an unusual octagonal design. At the top are twenty-four alternating triangles; on the side nearest the wall (and hidden from view), a cross wrapped by a serpent—a symbol linked to Moses, who nailed a serpent to a staff in the desert to fight off the plague. It is also an alchemical symbol. The writer Philip Gardiner points out that this depiction of the serpent descending the cross is rare, and suggests the symbolic meaning:

> The downward serpent is normally a Gnostic device and the downward pointing triangle forces the impression here, with two pointing upwards – giving the all-important 'balance' required to ascend. However, before the spirit or the higher nature can be freed or can rise, we must visit those places 'below' in the lower nature of man (lust, greed etc) and destroy them – hence the 'crushing' of the serpent underfoot. The serpent is duality, it is both kill and cure, it is good and evil, in this respect it points to our lower self which must be 'crucified' upon the cross, which is in the image.

Above the font high on the north wall is the old Templar cross originally sited somewhere outside the church, or perhaps at the point of the roof. Closer examination of the centre of the cross reveals a hand with the first two fingers raised making the sign of the blessing.

The slight curve of the wall to the right of the arch indicates that it would have been part of the original round church. On the inner left-hand capital is sited one of the most enigmatic Templar carvings: a green man—or what is commonly described as a green man. Some have suggested that its unique design is more like the horned god, perhaps the Celtic Cernunnos, a god of fertility, associated with serpents.

A common motif in English churches, the 'green man' name is particular to England, though similar figures can be found in Europe with different descriptions. For instance in France they may be called *masques de feuilles* (leaf masks) *or masques feuillus* (foliate masks). They usually have foliage around

Above A Templar cross on the interior north wall, originally sited outside, perhaps at the gable end.
Below left The octagonal font with its descending serpent symbol.
Below right The Garway 'green man, sited on the north capital of the interior arch. It has been suggested he may represent Cernunnos, a pagan deity associated with serpents.

them, often streaming from their mouth. Their precise origins are unknown, but they probably stem from old pagan idols that were incorporated into the fabric of the church.

The ceiling in the western half of the church is very unusual: barrelled in wood, it is inlaid with twenty-four six-pointed white stars.

The step beneath the arch is made from a reused grave slab; such slabs have been used throughout the church, and are most likely Templar. The practical explanation for such recycling is simply that the slabs are useful as building material. But an alternative view is suggested by the fact that old stone crosses are occasionally found embedded in churches where they have no structural purpose—they seem to be used to add 'power' to the structure. Either explanation (or both) may be valid.

From the grave slab step to the altar, the floor is laid with intricate medieval tiles.

Eastwards through the arch lies the simple stone altar, which was apparently hidden during Henry VIII's Reformation—quite a common practice at this time, the head of the new Church of England being intent on destroying evidence of its Catholic rival. In many churches throughout the country, figures were turned face down, disguised as paving slabs—or even a bridge, as in the case of the South Witham effigy (see page 152)—later to be restored to their proper place.

Down a step to the right of the altar is the Templars' chapel, in which they would have been initiated into the Order. An ancient wooden chest stands at the side with an explanatory notice: 'South chapel: 12th cent, note the piscina, arched with a trefoiled recess. Incised a fish, lamprey, chalice and host.' (A lamprey is a small eel-like fish, a delicacy in Templar times—this carving is indistinct, though, and may be a serpent.)

The carving above the piscina is particularly mysterious—it seems almost hieroglyphic, and is repeated in the porch of Aslackby church in Lincolnshire.

Another Templar tomb lid has been pressed into service, as the lintel in the south window in this chapel—the sword and floriated circular design are just discernible. This would have been an addition in the rebuilding of the chapel, which took place in the sixteenth century.

Above the west door of the chapel is the carving of a sponge, spear, sword, Tau cross, crown and three nails—a common medieval assembly of the items associated with the Crucifixion of Christ, found in many churches.

The tower and passageway are now kept locked; church staff are, however, able to allow access to this area. Points of interests within the passageway and tower are the tomb lid reused as a lintel, and a large wooden chest probably made by the Templars.

Below left Templars' chapel piscina, above which are carvings of a fish (left) and eel or snake (right). The central motif is similar to the winged sun disc of ancient Egyptian mythology. A very similar carving can be found in the porch of St Andrew's, Aslackby.
Below right An ancient wooden chest in the Templars' chapel.
Bottom left Tiled floor of the chancel.
Bottom right The ancient altar, hidden during the Reformation. Now restored.

✠ HEREFORD CATHEDRAL

The Templars built one of their round churches in Hereford, of which nothing remains except an echo in the name of Templars Lane on a street close to the centre of the city. A more tangible—and in fact unique—monument can be found in the cathedral, on the tomb of Thomas de Cantilupe: the carved images of fourteen Templar knights, in poses of mourning. They are lamenting the death of a man who was to have an extraordinary fate, one that throws light on religious thought of the period.

The connection between Thomas de Cantilupe and the Templars is unclear; some say he was a provincial governor for the Order, which would have been possible without being a full knight. But it is perhaps more likely that he was a valued supporter of the Order, and the carved knights on his tomb are there to remind the Templars to pray for him.

Thomas was chancellor to Henry III and held many important ecclesiastical posts, including Bishop of Hereford, before his death in 1282, but his immortal distinction was to be canonised—the last English saint before the Reformation.

The circumstances of his canonisation are covered in Robert Bartlett's book *The Hanged Man*. In 1307 three papal commissioners were given the task of judging Cantilupe's saintliness, and came to Hereford to hear testimony. The process was similar to a trial, with witnesses giving statements about alleged miracles associated with the candidate that would prove their fitness for sainthood. One particular miracle is the focus of Bartlett's book: the survival—or perhaps the resurrection—of a 'Welsh brigand', William Cragh, who lived close to Llanmadoc. At the time of this miracle Thomas Cantilupe had been dead for around ten years.

Above The tomb of St Thomas de Cantilupe. **Below** Detail of the south side of the tomb. The knights are said to be a reminder to the Templars to pray for Thomas' soul.

Lady Mary de Briouze gave testimony that William had been captured by her husband, the lord of the manor, had been sentenced to death and hanged. While suspended, he had voided his bowels and bladder, taken as signs of death.

Above Detail of the north side of the tomb. It is thought the knights were 'defaced' during the Reformation when the destruction of the imagery of the old Catholic faith was encouraged.

His whole face was black and in parts bloody or stained with blood. His eyes had come out of their sockets and hung outside the eyelids and the sockets were filled with blood. His mouth, neck and throat and the parts around them and also his nostrils were filled with blood, so that it was impossible ... for him to breathe. His tongue hung out of his mouth ... completely black and swollen and thick with blood sticking to it.

Lady Mary then testified that she took pity on the man and prayed to Thomas de Cantilupe of blessed memory to 'give him life', a tall order that came to pass, and later William went to Thomas's tomb in Hereford Cathedral to thank him. The canonisation judges were suitably impressed, and found in Thomas's favour.

It must be said that the acquisition of a saint was also a commercial boost for the town involved; pilgrims would start flocking to the shrine—St Hugh in Lincoln, St Thomas in Canterbury, and so on, and now St Thomas in Hereford ... a town without a saint would always be in the market for one.

✠ LUDLOW CASTLE

(SHROPSHIRE) *This site is important in relation to the Templars not so much for what it is, but for what it represents. Within the castle is a remarkable, well-preserved early Norman chapel dedicated to St Mary Magdalene, which may not even have been associated with the Templars (though the interior carvings include two Templar crosses, and the saint is their particular favourite). But it has a round nave and, as such, gives a good idea of what the small Templar 'round' churches would have looked like before they were lost—as at Dover, Hereford and Bristol.*

Above Two carved heads from the chapel interior.
Above right The Chapel of St Mary Magdalene from the west. Its association with the Templars is unclear although many older historical texts do describe it as a Templar chapel.
Right Originally a small chancel was attached to the chapel.
Opposite top East arch and arcading.
Opposite bottom left Western entrance to the chapel.
Opposite bottom right Columns and capitals of the eastern arch. The internal structure – now lost – would have been made of wood.

IN SEARCH OF THE KNIGHTS TEMPLAR

WALES AND THE BORDERS : LUDLOW CASTLE

✝ LLANMADOC

(GOWER) *Long before the early Christians came to this remote, wind-swept peninsula, it was home to a host of prehistoric settlers, who often left evidence of their lives in the caves that riddle the region—Paviland Cave housed the famous 'Red Lady', the oldest remains of a modern human yet discovered in Britain. All those ancient cultures would have had their sacred places, where they communed with gods and spirits—places that would be venerated too by later inhabitants. Llanmadoc Church was built in such a place, imbuing it with Christian holiness, and providing an ideal site for the Templars' own church.*

Opposite above Below the south window in the nave, the fifth-century stone, a remnant of the early Christian church of Llanmadoc.

Opposite below Four crosses atop Llanmadoc Church; the second from right is very similar to the one at Garway in Herefordshire.

Below The church of St Madoc looking northeast, out to sea.

Llanmadoc lies at the western end of the Gower peninsula, on a road that comes to a dead end after passing the church, which was built on high ground with panoramic views of the sea—perhaps it was this dramatic spectacle that drew people here. (The Gower itself was to be recognised by a much later culture as Britain's first Area of Outstanding Natural Beauty.)

Early Christian churches were often established on the site of cemeteries;—the grave of an important person would be a focus for further interments, and the burial ground would grow in importance. Local people would gather there for festivals to honour the dead, and in time a building would be established to give a more permanent base.

Llanmadoc Church grew up during the fifth century, one of the first Christian sites in Wales, as attested by a memorial stone found embedded in the wall of the rectory in 1861 (and now in the church). The Latin inscription reads: …VECTI FILIVS GVAN HIC IACIT ('of …vectus son of Guanus he lies here'), a formula typical of the fifth century. The church was dedicated to—perhaps even founded by—St Madoc (*llan* is Welsh for 'church'). Exactly who this saint was is unclear; he may have been St Aidan, the Irish saint, Madoc being an alternative Irish name for Aidan.

The early Christian Celtic community existed until the coming of the

Anglo-Normans—after the suppression of much of England, the conquerors turned west, in 1106 killing the last prince of the Gower, Hywel ap Goronwy. Henry, Earl of Warwick, then acquired the peninsula and built Swansea Castle. In 1156 Henry's wife Margaret granted the 'vil' (settlement) and church of Llanmadoc to the Templars. This was not a preceptory and is described as 'manor and church'. It was administered by Garway some sixty miles away (more than two days' travel at that time).

The basic fabric of the church that stands today was constructed during the Templars' lifespan, though exactly how much they influenced its design is not known. The interior, in common with other Norman churches, would have been vividly painted—when the later rector, J.D.

Davis, supervised the restoration in the 1860s, he noticed on the plaster hacked from the walls previously hidden texts and designs. At this time, the Reverend Davis—evidently a skilled carpenter—made the altar and pulpit himself.

Evelyn Lord casts an interesting light on contemporary reactions to the Templars' suppression. She describes how the Sheriff of Carmarthen and his men were sent to arrest the knights and seize their property, but were evidently in no hurry. They took all of three days, charging by the day—by the time they reached Llanmadoc, the cost of their services was almost as much as the property was able to generate in a year.

After the suppression the lands were transferred, along with the preceptory at Garway, to the Knights Hospitaller, who ran it from their commandery at Dinmore, Herefordshire. The Hospitallers held this estate until the Reformation and their dissolution in 1540.

Above left Detail of one of the two ancient marker stones set in the interior west wall.
Above right A marker stone, a cross with crosslets, similar to some of the carvings at Garway.
Right The west end of St Madoc's; the two old stones can be seen set into the wall.

IN SEARCH OF THE KNIGHTS TEMPLAR

In 1860 the diarist Francis Kilvert described the church as being in poor condition—'meaner than the meanest hovel in the village'—and the church warden, George Holland, confirmed this: 'Very much out of repair. The roof is not secured. Doors very much out of repair. Pews in most dilapidated condition. Earth allowed to lie against walls...' and so on, a catalogue of ruination.

Funds were raised and the church was restored, with the reopening ceremony on 26 April 1866. This also reopened old disputes, the 'ritual and style' of the ceremony causing much consternation among the Protestant community, worried that the church was being abducted back to the Catholic times of the Templars. In his guidebook to the church, F.G. Cowley says the rituals performed within the church were seen as 'a sinister threat to the Protestant establishment of evangelical Gower'. The debate raged for months.

Below left The altar, made from wood by the Reverend J.D. Davis in the 1860s. Depicted are the four evangelists with their respective symbols. From left to right, Luke – Ox, Matthew – Angel, Mark – Lion and John – Eagle.
Below right St Madoc's interior looking east.
Bottom left The wooden pulpit, also made by the Reverend J.D. Davis.
Bottom right St Madoc's looking west.

SCOTLAND

WHILE THE TEMPLARS undoubtedly had considerable estates in Scotland, the exact extent of their holdings is uncertain. Of the two incontestable records of Templar properties, the 1185 'inquest', or inventory, applied only to England, and the inventory held after their arrest did not happen in Scotland. Most Scottish records have been lost or destroyed. Transcripts of the trial give some indication but, as only two knights from Scotland were present, the accounts are limited. ✠ Scotland was the only country to pass no legislation enforcing the suppression decreed by the Pope in 1312 – indeed, the Templars were never officially annulled here. The English king, Edward II, had more pressing matters to deal with, locked in a conflict with Scotland that would end at Bannockburn. Refugees from France and England could therefore find sanctuary with their brothers in Scotland, staying at the more distant Templar houses or seeking refuge in the remote regions of the Western Isles. ✠ Few tangible traces of the Templars' presence remain. There is a modern monument to the Order at Maryculter, one of their main preceptories, near Aberdeen. Ancient ruins are still visible at the Templars' first preceptory, Ballentradoch, now the village of Temple in Midlothian, while Moffat's shell of a chapel in Dumfries and Galloway hangs on to existence. Two sites on the western seaboard, Kilmory and Kilmartin, display the grave slabs typical of this area, among them memorials to legendary knights who, it is said, arrived here in the early fourteenth century. ✠ The most spectacular site in Scotland associated with the Templars is the famous Rosslyn Chapel and its fantastic, mysterious carvings – given new prominence by *The Da Vinci Code*. It was built nearly 140 years after the official suppression and, while Templar connections are hotly debated, the Order in Scotland did indeed continue in some form, either absorbed into the Hospitallers or in their own right—a charter of King James IV, dated 19 October 1488, mentions lands that continued to belong to an order of Templars. ✠

✝ BALLENTRADOCH/TEMPLE

(MIDLOTHIAN) *The remains of a church in a deserted grave-yard, lying secluded in a quiet valley, and a single lonely archway in a remote field: all that stands of the Templars' first and greatest preceptory in Scotland, their headquarters for the lifetime of the Order, from where they administered their many other estates. A gift from the Scottish king, its very name proclaimed their martial role—in the Celtic language, Baile nan Trodach means 'stead of the warriors'. Its later name, Temple, is equally apposite if less resonant.*

Previous page The solitary arch that stands at the back of Temple village—the last remaining trace of the preceptory.
Above left Ballentradoch Templars' church from the southeast. At the point of the roof on the bell tower can be found carved graffiti, interpreted as VAESAC MIHM or VAESACN MIHM, the meaning and date of which are unknown.
Above right A small Templar cross at the apex of the western end of the church, which was built on some of the first land the Order received in Britain.

King David I granted the Templars 'the manor and chapel of Balantradoch' in 1153. Successive monarchs followed his example, until the Order owned substantial properties throughout Scotland—as Alfred Coutts says in his book *The Knights Templar in Scotland*, 'from Galloway to Aberdeenshire'. Coutts details some of these royal gifts:

> Malcolm IV, king of Scotland 1141–1165... donated a complete homestead in every burgh [borough] throughout the kingdom.
> William the Lion (1165–1214)... gifted the knights the barony of Maryculter, comprising of 8,000 acres.
> Alexander I, II, III, Robert I, II, James I, III, IV confirmed and increased the estates of the Templars from the royal exchequer.

Members of the nobility were known to bestow gifts on the Order too, known naturally enough as 'Templar lands'.

After the Order was suppressed, in 1312, all its properties were supposed to be handed over to the Hospitallers, whose chief Scottish seat was at

IN SEARCH OF THE KNIGHTS TEMPLAR

Torphichen in West Lothian. However, the Pope's edict was frequently not followed to the letter, if at all. In any case, the old Templar church continued to serve the parish, enduring for centuries before falling into ruin a hundred years ago.

✠ THE RUINED CHURCH stands just to the west of the village, in the valley of south Esk, next to the River Esk, which can be heard from inside the church. It dates from the early fourteenth century—the late Gothic tracery can still be seen, with animals carved at the ends of the mouldings above the windows.

There is no hard evidence to prove that Templars were buried in the churchyard. Many gravestones, though, bear a carved skull and crossbones—a familiar reminder of death, of course, but also a symbol associated with the Templars (and, more commonly, with the Masons). There are other Masonic symbols here too, such as a trowel (the symbol of the builder) and an egg timer (to symbolise the passing of time, or the impermanence of

Below Looking out of the church northwards, the recess at the bottom right would originally have held a tomb.

life), along with the classic compass and set square, as well as various cryptic inscriptions yet to be deciphered.

The headstones of local villagers also have their interest, among them the

Above left The gravestone of John Craig, a local farmer, who died in 1742.
Above right The piscina, to the right of the eastern end of the church.
Below Two views of the only relic from Temple preceptory.

memorial to the farmer at Outerston, John Craig, who died in 1742. He is shown wearing his best clothes and with his children. Sir William Gillies (1898–1973), the painter, lived and worked in Temple at No. 14 Main Street.

With no roof, the church's interior remains open to the elements. The west end of the ruin was the main entrance; at the east end the altar would have stood and, to the right of this, a carved piscina has survived. Various niches are visible in the walls, once used for tombs but now empty. What remains of the windows shows that they would have been ornate and substantial.

The only other Templar relic, the solitary preceptory arch, stands stark in a field to the east of the village. Poignantly, it was originally the main entrance to the Templars' manor house.

One Templar preceptor of Ballentradoch features in the unhappy story of Christiane of Esperston. Christiane's husband William selfishly decided to convey the ownership of their house to the Templars in return for rent, on which he could live a life of ease. He then suddenly died, leaving his wife and children without the means to survive. Accompanied by some 'men', the Templar preceptor called to take possession of the house, dragging out poor Christiane as she clutched at the door. Angry at the delay, one of the men took his sword and cut off her fingers, and threw her from the house.

She then went to Newbattle Abbey, where Edward I happened to be staying, and made her case to him. He was impressed and ordered that her property should be returned to her. When, shortly after, war broke out she was again evicted so her son Richard went to the then Templar Grand Master, the infamous Brian de Jay, for help. Brian agreed, on condition that Richard act as a guide for some Welsh troops whom he, Brian, was commanding in preparation for the Battle of Falkirk. Richard was caught in what was evidently a trap and was killed by the Welsh troops, apparently acting on Brian's command.

This story seems so untypical of any other accounts of the Templars that it is tempting to believe it is based on an anti-English legend of the poor Scottish widow being thrown from her house. But, according to Evelyn Lord, the story is probably factual and it is Brian de Jay who is untypical of the Templars (though the Ballentradoch preceptor was hardly a perfect knight himself).

Interestingly, as Baigent and Leigh record, Brian was one of the few Templars who were accused of heresy by name at the trial. He had been killed at Falkirk, but was quoted by one brother, Thomas Tocci de Thoroldeby, as having said that 'Christ was not the true God, but a mere man.'

Below Many Masonic tombstones can be found around Temple Church, the skull and crossbones being a common motif.

✝ KILMARTIN

(ARGYLL AND BUTE) *A remote land made for legend and drama: high mountains covered in mist, a rocky, rugged coastline, abundant rivers and sea lochs, sheltered glens—and traces of human habitation stretching back five thousand years and more. Kilmartin is rich in standing stones, henges, barrows and cairn burials, while nearby Temple Wood houses three stone circles thought to be a prehistoric ritual site. Its name concurs with medieval legends about the Templars fleeing after the suppression to the western seaboard of Scotland, where at least some of them found a final resting place in the graveyard of Kilmartin Church.*

Below left The entrance to the covered area within Kilmartin graveyard. The tomb used as a lintel reads 'heir lyis Mr Neil Cambel and Cristiane...'
Below right The skull and crossbones, an archetypal symbol pre-dating the Templars—it was used in the early Christian catacombs. It was said to be adopted by the Templars although no version attributable to the Order survives. The symbol was certainly used by freemasonry and this example is from one of the many Masonic graves found at Kilmartin.

Those legends started soon after the end of the Order, and have persisted for centuries. The wilder parts of Ireland were similarly reputed to be a refuge from the king's men—and excavations at the castle in Newcastle West in Co. Limerick have revealed evidence of the Templars indeed occupying the site after the suppression.

The suggestive evidence in Kilmartin's graveyard lies in the medieval grave slabs there—like those of Kilmory some eighteen miles to the south . A grave slab differs from a vertical gravestone in that it was intended for the top of a tomb, and would lie horizontally. Templar burials were in tombs, as gravestones were rarely used in their era. Where the Templars were known to have continued after the suppression under other names, the grave slabs they produced are very similar to the ones here.

As well as the medieval slabs, there are a number of later Masonic gravestones; some indicated by the skull and crossbones, a symbol also associated with the Templars. The fact that many of the later stones are Masonic—and many such Masonic burials can be found at former Templar churches, particularly in Scotland—does not mean that the Templars evolved into Masons. All that can be said with certainty is that these Masons had a retrospective interest in the Templars.

Above left Early medieval grave slabs with enigmatic designs, which were reused in 1707 and 1712.
Above right Looking south from Kilmartin graveyard.

While some grave slabs remain in the graveyard, the most interesting have been collected together under a glass-roofed stone outhouse. The older slabs are particularly valuable — they provide an accurate visual record of a medieval knight's weapons and dress, which were not described in great detail in the written record. Similar information can be gleaned from the depictions of tools and ships. (See also Kilmory, page 226.)

✝ THESE GRAVE SLABS have been arranged chronologically around the room, starting from the left of the entrance, ranging from about 1300 up to the early eighteenth century. The method of dating seems to be that those with the least ornamentation are the earliest, and those with the most are the latest. Usually this seems correct, although a couple of stones appear out of place. The two slabs positioned as the latest are dated 1707 and 1712, but they have clearly been recycled: the dates are crudely carved in a completely different style to the rest of the decorations, which would appear to be early medieval.

This reusing of old slabs is clear elsewhere, as in the slab dedicated to Iain Caimbeul.

The first slabs are simple in form, with just a sword. Moving on, the symbols start to become more intricate, and gain a foliated design in a Scandinavian style. The sword becomes less dominant and other motifs appear, suggesting the occupation of the deceased, such as shears. The design of the shears is typical of the latest tools developed by the Cistercians and the Templars.

The knights, facing forward, are similar in dress. They wear the thigh-length chain-mail coat, the hauberk, sometimes standing with a spear in the right hand but always with a sword positioned across the body to be drawn with the right hand. Every knight appears to have been right-handed, and it is known that spiral staircases in castles were designed to be defended by right-handed soldiers. It would follow that all soldiers were trained to fight right-handed whether this was natural to them or not. The only other detail of clothing readily identifiable is the pointed helmet.

Left Grave slab with the etched name of Iain Caimbeul and Duntroon (a local castle). The writing was clearly added at a later date when the slab was reused for Caimbeul — the Gaelic version of Campbell, the most powerful clan in Argyll.
Right Templar grave slab from Tomar, Portugal. This and many other Templar grave slabs show distinct similarities with fourteenth-century slabs from this area of Scotland.

IN SEARCH OF THE KNIGHTS TEMPLAR

Right Detail from a
Kilmartin grave slab: a
knight stands beneath what
appears to be a banner of
some kind. Note the thigh-
length chain mail overcoat,
the hauberk, standard
defensive wear for early
medieval knights.

Far right and below right
Examples of Kilmartin grave
slabs found in the covered
area of the churchyard.

Below A simple carved
sword is all that identifies
this slab as that of a knight.
The sword was so valuable
in the time of the Templars
that its worth was similar
to a substantial house.

✠ KILMORY

(ARGYLL AND BUTE) *The medieval chapel at Kilmory stands on the banks of Loch Sween, just as it meets the sea. These sea lochs, forming natural harbours, would have been convenient entry points for fugitive Templars sailing from France at the time of the suppression, and joining any British brothers also finding refuge in this wild and remote region. Whether they tried to re-establish their Order or, by contributing their skills, were assimilated into the local population, is not known; what is known, though, is that grave slabs depicting knights were not in use here until the early fourteenth century.*

Kilmory itself, once a deserted village, is now being repopulated. It lies about eighteen miles to the south of Kilmartin, which also houses an intriguing collection of grave slabs (see page 222). These slabs are found throughout the

Above The small chapel of Kilmory stands at the end of a narrow peninsula.

west coast and islands of Scotland, territory controlled by the Lords of the Isles—rulers so powerful that they were virtually independent of the Scottish Crown. The grave slabs in Kilmory, collected together in the chapel, were carved in a variety of styles by artists from both the local area and elsewhere, working from the fourteenth to the sixteenth centuries. The stone used seems to have been quarried from local sources, somewhere between here and Castle Sween, a few miles to the north.

Grave slabs were, fittingly, carved to reflect the occupation of the deceased in life—shears for a sheep farmer, hammer and anvil for a smith, for example—or, in the case of Templars and other religious people, his vocation. Sometimes there could be a blurring of the two. There are also carvings of boats, which may have several connotations: the importance of sea-power in this region of natural harbours, and hence an allegiance to the Lords of the Isles with their fleets of galleys; the seafaring adventures of local men, such as Henry St Clair (see Rosslyn Chapel, page 232); and, perhaps, a memory of those French refugees.

As well as grave slabs, the chapel displays early Christian stones, showing that there was a community here before AD 1000. There is also a single stone with an incised cross pattée, the only monument that was not originally found in Kilmory.

✠ THE GRAVE SLABS are arranged in the chapel in mostly chronological order, the earliest being to the left of the entrance. As at Kilmartin, the slabs give a powerful impression of medieval life and death.

IN SEARCH OF THE KNIGHTS TEMPLAR

Above The life-size sculpted grave slabs of knights, arranged under the frosted glass roof, give the chapel a supernatural atmosphere.

Far left The stone cross pattée, identified as Templar by Baigent and Leigh.

Left Two examples of Kilmory knights' grave slabs.

Above Two later grave slabs move away from the solitary sword design and start to accrue more details of the owners' profession, such as boats, swords, shears and other motifs.

Above right Eventually the slabs dispense with weapons altogether and give prominence to articles such as shears and a hammer.

Opposite These two carvings of fourteenth-century knights from Kilmory retain their fine detail, having been worked from hard stone and surviving away from common sources of erosion such as acid rain.

Right The so-called Macmillan's Cross, carved locally for Alexander Macmillan, keeper of Castle Sween in the late fifteenth century. It shows the Crucifixion on one side, with the Virgin Mary on the left and St John on the right. On the other side, a hunting scene has been neatly carved into the available space. Like many of the grave slabs, the cross was originally positioned in the church-yard; its base is still in place, at the west end.

✠ MOFFAT

(DUMFRIES AND GALLOWAY) *A little-known relic from Templar history, lost to the wider world but recorded in the town archives: the ruins of a chapel, dedicated to St Cuthbert, dating back to a time when the Order had extensive holdings in the region, close to an old Roman road. The chapel served a Templar 'hospital' for travellers, which, along with other structures in the settlement, has long been obliterated. But the barest shell of the chapel clings on amid the scenic Moffat hills, built into a house within a working farm named after this medieval remnant.*

Those early travellers would have been taking the north–south route from Carlisle to Glasgow and Edinburgh. To get to the main road, they could take the old track—a 'hollow way' worn in the ground by constant use—that runs west of the town past the chapel. The hospital itself stood just off the Roman road; here the Templars carried on the monastic tradition of caring for travellers, providing accommodation as well as medical attention. Today the chapel stands on private land, though the owners do allow access.

IN SEARCH OF THE KNIGHTS TEMPLAR

Opposite The western
arch of St Cuthbert's Chapel.
Above The eastern end
of the chapel, which would
tradtionally have held the
altar; unusually, it shows
a bricked-up entrance.
The western end has no
entrance, suggesting that
the chapel may have been
orientated to the west.
Left Looking east over the
town of Moffat to Craig Fell.

✝ ROSSLYN CHAPEL

(MIDLOTHIAN) *A medieval hologram carved in stone — a fantastic fusion of images both Christian and pagan: Rosslyn Chapel has been casting its spell for centuries, and now draws modern pilgrims intent on understanding its mysteries. It is believed by many to be a monument to the legacy of the Templars, knights who left few written records in their lifetime, and who would rectify this by influencing the construction of a library in stone.*

For all the wonder and speculation it has inspired, the chapel was founded, in 1446, from a thoroughly orthodox motive: one man, growing older, reflecting on his life and wanting to pay his dues to God. He was William St Clair, third and last Prince of Orkney and a knight of the Order of St James. He would devote the rest of his life — nearly forty years — to this very project.

William's family name has been standardised here to St Clair — it appears elsewhere as St Clare, St Cleer, Saint Clair, Saintclaire and Sinclair. The Norman St Clairs had a mixed heritage, including Viking through both the Dukes of Normandy and the jarls (Earls) of Orkney, and their scions had numerous adventures on land and sea. Several had fought at the Battle of Hastings, one of them, also called William, being a first cousin to the Conqueror himself.

William St Clair was in his early forties when he felt moved to begin his great work of devotion. As Hay's *Genealogie of the Saintclaires of Rosslyn* says, 'it came into his mind to build a house for God's service'. This 'house' would be a collegiate church, dedicated to St Matthew, built near his castle. Collegiate churches, often established with private funding, were run by an appointed body of men (the 'college'). They were founded for a variety of purposes: as centres of learning, to study theology, and as a place of worship whose officials and congregation would pray for the souls of the founding family.

Some saw a correlation between the magnificence of the church and the piety of the founder... certainly William was determined that his church would be 'of most curious work'. So that it might be 'done with greater glory and splendour he caused artificers to be brought from other regions and foreign kingdoms and caused daily to be abundance of all kinds of workmen present as masons, carpenters, smiths, barrowmen and quarriers...'

William would not stint — in money, energy, or imagination. He himself drew the designs of both chapel and decorations on wooden boards, which the masons copied.

For all his ambition, though, the structure was unfinished at his death in 1484. The

Below Rosslyn Chapel from the northwest. The steel roof was erected in 1997, in an attempt to arrest the deterioration of the external stonework, which had been left vulnerable to atmospheric pollution.

IN SEARCH OF THE KNIGHTS TEMPLAR

original plan shows that the chapel that exists today was to have been the eastern end of a far bigger church. Where the west door is now, it was planned to have a tower and beyond that a nave, whose foundations have been found and stretch 90 feet to the west. Two transepts were planned to make the church a cruciform shape.

The sacristy (where sacred objects are kept) at Rosslyn is, unusually, beneath the level of the church, more like a crypt. It is sited away from the church at the most eastern point, carved into the side of the hill, its eastern end containing a window and another altar. It is thought this vault may pre-date the chapel itself, because designs for the main building can be seen etched into the wall.

Fittingly, William was buried in his creation. It may not have reached the scale he had planned, but its interior reflected an unfettered imagination: every surface a dizzying riot of clashing cultures—orthodox Christian icons and older, wilder, pagan images: from Christ in his majesty to winged serpents gnawing at the Tree of Life, from a bewildering array of angels to a

Above The crypt/sacristy tomb. The transience of life and the presence of death are symbolised in this carving, behind which, etched on the wall, are plans for the main building, indicating that the sacristy may pre-date the chapel.

Top left East window of Rosslyn from the walkway. The steel structure that now surrounds the upper part of the chapel provides a unique opportunity to view details previously hidden.
Top right The south porch.
Above left Exterior detail of an announcing angel.
Above middle The western entrance to the chapel containing the baptistery and organ loft, added in 1881 by Francis Robert, 4th Earl of Rosslyn.
Above right Engrailed crosses atop the south railings—the cross of the St Clair family is identified by the serrated edge.

panoply of licentious green men and women. The human element is celebrated too, in the idiosyncratic St Clair family itself, especially William's seafaring grandfather—whose exploits may be the foundation of some of the most puzzling carvings found here. Also mysterious are what can be called graffiti; some have been described as 'masons' marks'—some definitely are, but many other marks are enigmatic and are definitely not.

Templar symbols have been identified here too—and the St Clairs' link with the Order is reputed to begin even before the church was in existence. Legend has it that their first Grand Master, Hugh de Payens, was married to a Katherine St Clair. After she died and Hugh was in his fifties, he 'took the cross' and went on Crusade, subsequently founding the Templars. Shortly after the Council of Troyes had given the Templars official papal recognition in 1128, Hugh came to Scotland as part of his visit to Britain. Temple village (see page 218), close to Rosslyn, was donated to the Order soon afterwards.

Rosslyn was certainly in keeping with one of the Templar legends of building tunnels and underground chambers. Beneath the chapel several vaults have been detected by scanners but, as yet, not fully explored. The one attempt to reveal the chapel's subterranean secrets was undertaken by Andrew Sinclair, a writer whose connection with the chapel is both familial and professional.

In 1997 Sinclair had the chapel surveyed using a ground-scanner, a non-invasive way of detecting any hollows or anomalies within the stonework. This detected the vaults, along with stairways. After removing some flagstones Sinclair entered one of the peripheral chambers, finding coffins and bones. He also established that the crypt had been sealed, making access to the main chambers impossible from the chamber he was in. He then turned to an 'industrial endoscope', to try to see what was inside the central chambers. This was lowered through a bore hole made by drilling; unfortunately the cavity repeatedly filled with dust and rubble, and the project was abandoned.

Sinclair seems to feel that this was, in a way, a respectable outcome; maybe he was being a little too nosy. The chambers along with the entombed Sinclair knights could continue to rest in peace.

During his investigations Sinclair also located a tunnel that went from the chapel to Rosslyn Castle, a distance of around 500 yards, which he described as 'huge and very deep underground'. Naturally, his discoveries fuelled rumours of hidden treasures — gold and precious jewels, or priceless sacred relics.

Above A carving said to support the Templar connection to Rosslyn Chapel – a knight in chain mail carrying a lance shares his horse with another who barely hangs on at the back. The similarity to the Templars' seal of two riders on one horse is clear.

Speculation apart, the very date of the chapel's foundation would seem to distance it from any direct involvement with the Templars—the Order had been suppressed nearly 140 years earlier. In fact, their relationship to Rosslyn is unclear, and hotly disputed to this day. The disbanded brothers could have regrouped to form another order, which did have an influence on the chapel; such an order may have resurfaced later as Freemasons. Or perhaps the influence was more subtle, transmitted through other knightly orders that ex-Templars are known to have joined. One such order was that of St James—of which the founder of Rosslyn, William St Clair, was a member.

The Knights of St James (or Santiago) were founded in the twelfth century in Spain, with the same goal as the Templars: to protect pilgrims, in this case travelling to Santiago de Compostela in northern Spain. The Order expanded and became instrumental in the re-conquest of the Iberian peninsula, driving out the Moors. The knights became specialists in maritime expeditions, developing the seafaring skills that would be passed to the great explorers—

Above Rosslyn Chapel interior looking east. The unique design can be seen in the way the altar is placed. Usually the main altar would be at the eastern end of a Christian church; here it is supplanted by the Lady Chapel with its profusion of foliage and angels.
Opposite top A grave slab said to be Templar; the eight-lobed circular design would support this attribution.

and incidentally inspiring one of the threads running through Rosslyn.

Knights of Santiago were claimed by gypsies to be their special protectors. Sir William St Clair, grandson of the chapel builder, honoured this tradition, allowing them sanctuary within the grounds of his castle, despite complaints that the family were harbouring outlaws. Gypsies gathered annually here to perform plays—which in their bawdiness and irreverence echoed the theme of nature worship evident in the chapel. They resembled traditional pagan seasonal festivals, with their strong links to fertility, some of which still survive: the 'Oss' in Padstow, Cornwall, or the 'Straw Bear' at Whittlesea, Cambridgeshire. The 'Oss' has Robin Hood as one of its main characters, dressed in Lincoln green—a metamorphosis of the original 'Green Man'. The gypsies' Mayday plays at Rosslyn also featured Robin, who, due to his subversive connotations, was banned at the time. The original Mayday festivals have been described as 'orgiastic'; according to Baigent and Leigh, the resulting offspring were called 'Robin's sons'—possibly the origin of Robinson.

IN SEARCH OF THE KNIGHTS TEMPLAR

What can be seen today encompasses the series of repairs and restorations carried out through the centuries as the fortunes of the chapel rose and fell—reglazing, for instance, and other weatherproofing methods. A more recent attempt at conservation has had an unfortunate effect. In 1954, in a misguided effort to 'preserve' the interior carvings, they were coated with a 'cementitous slurry', diligently and painstakingly applied. Not only has this affected the visual appearance of the carvings, it has also had a detrimental effect on the stone it was designed to protect, sealing in corrosive moisture.

Since 1997, when the steel roof seen today was erected to dry out the chapel, conservationists have been exploring how best to preserve the carvings; at some point in the future the cement coating is likely to be removed. Luckily, it does not detract from the beauty and mystery of the images.

With all its carvings of foliage and nature spirits, Rosslyn appears to celebrate the cyclical: death and rebirth. The 'green man': the symbol of the cyclical god, a dying god whose lifespan followed the seasonal cycle.

One of the best-known features is the Apprentice Pillar, its four curving organic strands climbing the column reminiscent of the DNA spiral. The pillar has become an iconic mystical symbol. Rosslyn has been described as a liminal place between two worlds, material and spiritual, and this pillar the threshold.

Its name comes from the Masonic tradition associated with Rosslyn, and tends to influence interpretation. This story tells of a master mason set the task of carving a particularly intricate column; he goes abroad for further study. In his absence, his apprentice does the job—perfectly. On his return, the master mason, outraged and jealous, kills the apprentice. The column is then named after the hapless young man. A carving elsewhere in the chapel is said to depict the apprentice himself, with a fatal wound on his forehead.

Below The grave slab of William de St Clair (1297–1330) He died in Spain fighting the Moors while taking the heart of the dead king, Robert the Bruce, on a crusade to Jerusalem. Robert the Bruce had long wished to go on a crusade and on his death his heart was given the chance, but it was way-laid in Spain by the Moors. Facing defeat, the Scottish knights hurled the Bruce's heart into the fray. They still lost, but the Moors, impressed by the knights' bravery, later returned the relic to the survivors.

Viewing the pillar as a representation of the 'tree of life', Yggdrasil in Norse mythology, might be more consistent with the symbology it represents and the elemental friction it depicts.

There has been much speculation about the column being hollow and containing some treasure or other: the Holy Grail again, or, less commonly, the mummified head of Christ. Until technology provides a non-invasive method of scanning the pillar that can differentiate between stone and organic matter, these questions will remain unanswered. Certainly no metal objects are embedded within it, as Andrew Sinclair found when he scanned the pillar during his 1997 survey.

Within the chapel are carvings of plants that are completely out of place in fifteenth-century Scotland, not just incongruent to the decoration of a chapel but, according to orthodox history, completely unknown to Europeans of the time.

America was to be officially discovered in 1492 by Christopher Columbus, a man who had absorbed the Templars' navigational legacy through his contact with the Knights of Christ in Portugal, from where he originally intended to set sail. But the seafaring skills of the Templars were also said to have been utilised by Prince Henry Sinclair (c. 1345–1400), the grandfather of Rosslyn's founder. He voyaged to the New World, and discovered and recorded its flora and fauna, later to be depicted on the walls of Rosslyn.

Henry organised a fleet of ships to sail around the northern coastline of the Atlantic, calling at Iceland, Greenland and then on to Canada, Nova Scotia (New Scotland), Newfoundland and New England. This was a major expedition with twelve ships. The motive was not idle curiosity; vast fortunes were being made at the time as trading links were established—a sack of spice could buy a house and servants.

For the expedition, he commissioned a map to be made by the Venetian Zeno brothers, Antonio and Nicolo. Antonio's account of the journey was published in 1558, and the map they made was to become known as the 'Zeno map.'

The members of the crew spent some months exploring Nova Scotia; Henry's visit is recorded in the legends of the Micmac Indians who lived there. They remember the men who came from the east and taught them to fish with nets.

Above A 'green man' found above the altar, the most holy place, usually reserved for the cross in a Christian church. He is the leader of over one hundred green men and women who populate the walls of Rosslyn.
Opposite far right
The magnificent, iconic symbol of Rosslyn, the Apprentice Pillar.
Opposite bottom left
Serpents at the base of the Apprentice Pillar, holding strands of hemp in their mouths that wind up, spiralling around the pillar, creating an eternal tension.

Small pictures opposite, clockwise from top left
A feathered crouching angel in the Lady Chapel; a carving said to be the bearer of the Grail; the fallen angel, bound with ropes, identified by some as Lucifer, cast out from heaven; Sacristy angel; the internal north wall showing a mother, child and the devil. The devil appears to be secretly drawing the child away from the mother; Lady Chapel lion.

In Nova Scotia a medieval Venetian cannon was found in Louisburg harbour, and a rock carving in Massachusetts of a knight bearing the coat of arms of the Clan Gunn from Scotland. On Rhode Island is the 'Newport tower', an eight-pillared structure bearing a strong resemblance to the round churches of the Templars. The local Indians said the tower was built by 'fire-haired men with green eyes who sailed up river in a ship like a gull with a broken wing.'

Prince Henry was killed in an ambush in Orkney soon after returning from the trip, and his son, also called Henry, was abducted and imprisoned for fifteen years. The enterprising St Clairs seem to have made some powerful enemies. Conscious of the danger, Henry's grandson William decided to stay closer to home in Scotland and eventually gave his attention to the design and construction of Rosslyn Chapel.

Henry St Clair's voyage was connected to the Scottish Templars, just as, at the same time, the Portuguese voyages of discovery under Henry the Navigator were connected to the Portuguese Templars.

In Portugal the Templars had evolved into the Knights of Christ and established a tradition of exploration of ever further lands, the red Templar cross pattée prominently displayed on their sails. They effectively created the Portuguese empire. It is likely that the Templars who arrived in Scotland developed in a similar way, but clandestinely and without royal patronage, and were therefore unrecognised by history.

They brought with them the knowledge of navigation and map making learnt from contact with Islam, including a new form of map called a 'portolan'—a graphic representation of past journeys, incrementally gathered, giving the seaman detailed charts of the coast as the ship went from port to port.

IN SEARCH OF THE KNIGHTS TEMPLAR

A famous example of a portolan is the 'Piri Reis map', which shows Africa and America with incredible precision but was drawn in 1513. Reis was an admiral, but also a known pirate, and was executed for losing a critical battle. Most known maps that pre-date Reis's are similar to the Mappa Mundi, a land-based view of the world, often with Jerusalem in the centre, useless for navigation on a boat.

✙ ROSSLYN CHAPEL does indeed deserve its description as a liminal space between the material and spiritual, but, other elements collided here: the seafarers' traditions with the land-based fertility cults, the Viking clans with Norman aristocracy, the ancient pagan beliefs with the 'new' religion of Christianity, all crashing in a vortex recorded in stone. A crossroads too, for the legacy and symbolism of the Templars which makes its last appearance in the medieval world, later to be absorbed into the traditions of Masonic ritual also found at Rosslyn.

From the simple, pious ambitions of nine knights centuries before, the Templars created a material and spiritual presence that swept through their age. Their traditions and symbolism remain mysterious, but here at Rosslyn that symbolism is recorded: a codex for the modern researcher to decipher, trying to get close to the medieval mind of William St Clair and the vision of the Knights Templar.

Appendix: *The Alignment of Templar Churches*

Towards the end of researching this book, I discovered an interesting feature of the Templars' sacred buildings. While Christian churches are traditionally aligned east–west, with the altar in the east – probably an echo of a much earlier, pagan practice related to the power of the rising sun – those Templar churches and chapels I measured seem to be aligned to the north of east, in a range of some 10 to 35 degrees.

The archaeologist St John Hope had noticed an 'incorrect' alignment of the Templars' round church in his 1901 survey of the Temple Bruer site. He did not elaborate on the point, though the mere fact that he chose to make it shows that it was thought unusual. In devotion to their religion, church builders would presumably strive to make as perfect an east–west alignment as possible, yet in medieval times this was evidently not always the case.

A number of possibilities could be suggested to account for the variation. Sloppy building techniques would have given imprecise results, but this theory can be discounted due to the consistent northeast bias – generally careless work would have produced variations to the south as much as to the north. In any case, it is unlikely that the masons who laid the ground plan for a building would be guilty of such an error; they, and their builders, had the sun to guide them, in the same way as it helped them to navigate (along with the stars) and order their calendar.

It is also possible that the Templars – with experienced sailors in their Order – introduced the compass into their methods for orientating sacred buildings, and it was irregularities in this method that produced the skew to the north. Significantly, one of the Templars' keenest supporters, the Bishop of Acre, Jacques de Vitry, was one of the first westerners to comment on the use of a compass for navigation. In 1218 he noted during a sea voyage that an iron needle will continue to point towards the pole star after being magnetised by a lodestone. But, although intriguing, no other evidence would bear out the use of a compass for alignment, and in fact many Templar buildings were built before its known introduction in the West.

The most persuasive theory for churches and chapels being off the exact east–west line is the theory of 'patronal alignment': at a given location, the building will be aligned towards the position in which the sun rises on the morning of the feast day of the saint to whom the church is dedicated. There have been some studies of this feature in non-Templar churches, and enough is known for the principle to be broadly accepted; although the study of this phenomenon is very new, and many church historians are unaware that it even exists.

It is not always known to which saint Templar churches were dedicated, and the patronal alignment principle could well be indicative. The London Temple, for example, is aligned 16 degrees to the north of east. Taking into account changes in the calendar, and using AD 1200 as a given year, the sun would rise in line with the church in late August, around the 29th – the feast of John the Baptist, a saint whom the Templars were known to venerate especially. The round church at Dover's Western Heights also shares this alignment.

The feast day of Mary Magdalene, another favourite saint of the Templars, is held on 22 July, a day that would see the sun rise 33 degrees to the north of east – an alignment found at Ribston Chapel.

While the phenomenon of patronal alignment has not been sufficiently researched to create any standardised theories, it would be easy to compile a definitive list of the alignment of sacred Templar buildings, through Europe, and from this data work out the precise orientations. The alignments could substantiate claims that the Order held the highest esteem for Mary Magdalene and John the Baptist over all other saints. In an order that left little written records, architectural codes become doubly significant.

Site directions

A good map is recommended, and is essential for the more remote sites. Ordnance Survey (OS) coordinates have been given for each site.

The full postal address is usually given as well. For more detailed information, the postcode, as well as the OS coordinate, can be entered into web map services, such as:

Streetmap
www.streetmap.co.uk

Multimap
www.multimap.com
This can also give directions.

OS Get-a-map
www.ordnancesurvey.co.uk/oswebsite/getamap
An excellent service that gives large-scale results.

Google
www.maps.google.co.uk

If there is an admission charge to a site, this is noted, along with opening times. But readers should be aware that details may change without notice, so it is advisable to check before making a long journey. Contact numbers, email addresses and websites are given where possible, but these are not available for some sites, especially churches. These are indicated as 'Usually open' – that is, during a working day – along with details of any keyholder. A few sites are on private land, and may be viewed only from outside. Where there is access to private land, visitors are asked to act responsibly.

LONDON

✠ ALL HALLOWS BY THE TOWER [OS TQ333806]

Byward Street
London
EC3R 5BJ

TEL: (020) 7481 2928
FAX: (020) 7488 3333
EMAIL: parish@allhallowsbythe
tower.org.uk
www.allhallowsbythetower
.org.uk

Admission free.
• Opening times:
Monday–Friday 09.00–17.30;
Sunday 10.00–17.00;
Sunday service 11.00.
• Circle / District lines to Tower Hill.

✠ TEMPLE CHURCH [OS TQ312810]

Temple
London
EC4Y 7BB
TEL: (020) 7353 3470
EMAIL: verger@templechurch
.com
www.templechurch.com

Admission free.
• Generally open Wednesday–Sunday, but subject to change.
• Tubes within walking distance: Temple or Blackfriars (District and Circle lines); Chancery Lane (Central Line). Temple and Chancery Lane stations are closed on Sundays.
• For access to the Temple Church on Sundays, motorists and pedestrians enter the Temple via Tudor Street, off Bouverie Street (from Fleet Street) and Temple Avenue (from Embankment). Pedestrians may also enter the Temple from Fleet Street via Middle Temple Lane.

✠ TOWER OF LONDON [OS TQ335806]

London
EC3N 4AB
TEL: 0870 756 6060
www.hrp.org.uk/webcode
/tower_home.asp

Admission charge.
• Opening times: 1 March–31 October: Tuesday–Saturday 09.00–18.00; Sunday–Monday 10.00–18.00; last admission 17.00. 1 November–28 February: Tuesday–Saturday 09.00–17.00; Sunday–Monday 10.00–17.00; last admission 16.00.
• Circle / District lines to Tower Hill. Follow signs to the main entrance of the Tower.

THE SOUTHEAST

West Sussex

✛ SHIPLEY CHURCH
[OS TQ145218]

Church Close
Shipley RH13 8PJ
Usually open.

✛ SOMPTING CHURCH
[OS TQ161056]

Church Lane
Sompting BN15 0AZ
Usually open.

Kent

✛ TEMPLARS ROUND
CHURCH [OS TR313407]

Western Heights CT17 9DX

*Note: not shown on maps.
At the first roundabout
encountered on the outskirts of
Dover when approaching from
the A20 take the sign left to
'Western Heights', then the
next immediate right up the hill.
The ruined church is at the top
of the hill on the left, visible
from the road surrounded by
a staked fence.*

✛ STROOD TEMPLE
MANOR [OS TQ735687]

Knight Road
Strood ME2 2AB
TEL: (01634) 338110
EMAIL: visitor.centre@medway
.gov.uk
Admission free.
• *Open: 1 April–31 October,
Sunday only. Other times by
appointment only.*

✛ TEMPLE EWELL
CHURCH [OS TR285441]

Church Hill
Temple Ewell CT16 3DR

Usually open.

Essex

✛ CRESSING TEMPLE
[OS TL799187]

Witham Road
Braintree CM77 8PD
TEL: (01376) 584453
http://www.cressingtemple
.org.uk

Admission charge.
• *Cressing Temple barns opening
times: Easter Sunday–
30 September, Monday–Friday
09.30–16.30; Sunday
10.30–17.30.*

Berkshire

✛ BISHAM ABBEY
[OS SU846849]

Bisham Abbey National Sports
Centre
Near Marlow SL7 1RT
TEL: (01628) 476911

*Not open to the public. The
abbey can be viewed from over
the river, by taking the Thames
path (OS SU858861) from
Marlow, and walking west for
about a mile. This also gives good
views of the Norman church at
Bisham.*

Hampshire

✛ SELBORNE CHURCH
[OS SU740338]

Selborne Road
Selborne GU34 3JQ

Usually open.

Hertfordshire

✛ ROYSTON CAVE
[OS TL356407]

Melbourn Street
Royston SG8 7BT
TEL: (01763) 245484

Admission charge.
• *Opening times: Easter
weekend–September; Saturday,
Sunday and bank holidays only,
14.30–17.00.*

THE SOUTHWEST

Bristol

✛ TEMPLE CHURCH OF
THE HOLY SEPULCHRE
[OS ST593727]

Temple Street, off Victoria
Street BS1 6RD
No access to interior.

Somerset

✛ TEMPLECOMBE
CHURCH, ST MARY'S
[OS ST708227]

Church Hill
Templecombe BA8 0HG

Usually open.

Cornwall

✛ TEMPLE CHURCH,
ST CATHERINE OF
ALEXANDRIA
[OS SX146732]

Temple PL30 4HW

Usually open.

THE MIDLANDS

Cambridgeshire

✢ CAMBRIDGE ROUND CHURCH [OS TL448588]

Bridge Street
Cambridge CB2 1UB

Admission charge.
• Opening times:
Tuesday–Saturday 10.00–17.00;
Sunday and Monday
13.00–17.00.

✢ DENNY ABBEY
[OS TL489686]

The Farmland Museum
Ely Road
Waterbeach
Cambridge CB5 9PQ
TEL: (01223) 860988
EMAIL: f.m.denny@tesco.net
www.dennyfarmlandmuseum
.org.uk

Admission charge.
• Opening times: 1 April–31
October, daily 12.00–17.00.

✢ GREAT WILBRAHAM CHURCH OF ST NICHOLAS
[OS TL548577]

Church Street
Great Wilbraham CB1 5JQ

Usually open.

Leicestershire

✢ ROTHLEY [OS SK576123]

The Rothley Court Hotel
Westfield Lane
Rothley LE7 7LG
TEL: (0116) 237 4141
FAX: (0116) 237 4483
EMAIL: 6501@greeneking.co.uk
www.rothleycourt.com

Ask at reception for the key to
the chapel.

Oxfordshire

✢ SANDFORD
[OS SP531018]

Oxford Thames Four Pillars
    Hotel
Henley Road
Sandford-on-Thames
    OX4 4GX
TEL: (01865) 334444
EMAIL: thames@four-pillars.
    co.uk

Ask in reception for permission
to look around.

Warwickshire

✢ TEMPLE BALSALL CHURCH OF ST MARY THE VIRGIN [OS SP206759]

Fen End Road
Temple Balsall B93 0AN

Usually open.

LINCOLNSHIRE

✢ SOUTH WITHAM
Preceptory site
[OS SK928203]

Post Lane
South Witham NG33 5LB

This is north out of the town.

✢ TEMPLE BRUER
[OS TF008537]

(Preceptory tower)
Temple Lane
Temple Bruer LN5 0DG

Open at reasonable times. On
private land in a working farm.

✢ ASLACKBY
Preceptory site
[OS TF087302]

Temple Lane
Aslackby NG34 0HJ

✢ ANGEL, GRANTHAM
[OS SK913359]

The Angel & Royal Hotel
High Street
Grantham NG31 6PN
TEL: (01476) 565816
FAX: (01476) 567149
EMAIL: enquiries@angeland
    royal.co.uk
www.angelandroyal.com

Ask in reception for permission
to look around.

✢ BURTON UPON STATHER CHURCH OF ST ANDREW [OS SE870178]

High Street
Burton upon Stather
Scunthorpe DN15 9BP

Usually locked; key details and
phone numbers on notice board.

✢ LINCOLN CATHEDRAL
[OS SK978718]

Minster Yard, Lincoln LN2 1PX
TEL: (01522) 544544
www.lincolncathedral.com

Admission charge.
• Opening times: summer:
Monday–Friday 07.15–20.00,
Saturday and Sunday
07.15–18.00;
winter: Monday–Saturday
07.15–18.00,
Sunday 07.15–17.00.

✢ LINCOLN CASTLE
[OS SK974718]

Castle Hill, Lincoln LN1 3AA
TEL: (01522) 511068
FAX: (01522) 512150
EMAIL: Lincoln_Castle@
    lincolnshire.gov.uk
www.lincolncastle.com

Admission charge.
• Opening times:
Monday–Saturday 09.30–17.30,
Sunday 11.00–17.30. Winter:
closes at 16.00.

✢ CHURCH OF ST JOHN THE BAPTIST
[OS SK927193]

Church Street
South Witham NG33 5PL

Key to church available from
nearby cottage; details on notice
board at site.

✢ CHURCH OF ST JAMES THE GREAT
[OS TF084304]

Aveland Way
Aslackby NG34 0HH

Key to church available from
nearby cottage; details on notice
board at site.

YORKSHIRE

✠ PENHILL CHAPEL
[OS SE035887]

On the northern approach to Penhill Tor. Site is accessed on foot, half a mile up the path that starts from the A684 (OS SE032889), just past Temple Farm, where there is a lay-by. Footpath and chapel are signposted from the road.

✠ RIBSTON HALL
[OS SE391537]

Wetherby Road
Little Ribston LS22 4EZ

Not open to the public; chapel can be viewed by taking footpath around hall.

✠ TEMPLE HIRST
[OS SE596252]

Temple Manor Nursing Home
Temple Hirst
Selby YO8 8QJ

Not open to the public; can be viewed from the road.

✠ CHRIST CHURCH
[OS NZ664057]

High Street
Westerdale YO21 2DT

Usually open.

✠ CLIFFORD'S TOWER
[OS SE604514]

Tower Street
York YO1 9SA
TEL: (01904) 646940

Admission charge.
• *Opening times: 17 July–31 August, daily 09.30–19.00; 29 March–16 July and 1–30 September, daily 10.00–18.00; 1–31 October, daily 10.00–17.00; 1 November–31 March, daily 10.00–16.00.*

✠ BRIDGE [OS NZ662061]

Westerdale YO21 2DU

WALES AND THE BORDERS

Herefordshire

✠ GARWAY CHURCH OF ST MICHAEL [OS SO453224]

Garway HR2 8RJ

The church stands outside the village, and is not well signposted. About half a mile from the village on the road going west is a white house on the right, opposite a turning; take this turning into a lane. The church is a few hundred yards down this lane on the left.
  Usually open.

✠ HEREFORD CATHEDRAL [OS SO510397]

(Tomb of Thomas de Cantilupe)
5 College Cloisters
Cathedral Close
Hereford HR1 2NG
TEL: (01432) 374200
FAX: (01432) 374220
EMAIL: office@hereford
  cathedral.org
www.herefordcathedral.org

The tomb is in the northeast of the cathedral.

Shropshire

✠ LUDLOW CASTLE CHURCH [OS SO508746]

Castle Square
Ludlow SY8 1AX
TEL: (01584) 873355
EMAIL: info@ludlowcastle.com
www.ludlowcastle.com

Admission charge.
• *Opening times:*
January: weekends only 10.00–16.00; February–March: daily 10.00–16.00; April–July: daily 10.00–17.00; August: daily 10.00–19.00; September: daily 10.00–17.00; October–December: daily 10.00–16.00.

Gower

✠ LLANMADOC CHURCH [OS SS438934]

Llanmadoc SA3 1DE

Key available from house opposite, accessible at reasonable times.

SCOTLAND

Midlothian

✤ TEMPLE CHURCH
[OS NT314586]

Temple EH23 4SH

✤ ROSSLYN CHAPEL
[OS NT274630]

Roslin EH25 9PU
TEL: (0131) 440 2159
FAX: (0131) 440 1979
EMAIL: rosslynch@aol.com
www.rosslynchapel.org.uk

Admission charge.
• Opening times:
Monday–Saturday 09.30–17.00;
Sunday 12.00–16.45.

✤ PRECEPTORY ARCH
[OS NT318585]

High Street EH23 4SG

Park on Temple High Street; arch is at back of houses through obvious gap.

Argyll and Bute

It is essential to have a good map to find Kilmartin and, especially, Kilmory. Note: there are two places called Kilmory; the relevant site is in Argyll, not in the Highlands.

✤ KILMARTIN CHURCH
[OS NR834988]

Kilmartin PA31 8RN

Usually open.

✤ KILMORY CHAPEL
[OS NR703751]

No postcode.

Stands due south of Kilmartin. Travel first on the A816, after about a mile taking the right on to the B8025. Then travel roughly southwest along the banks of Loch Sween for around twenty miles, along a single-track road. On the approach to the chapel, it is signposted off the road to the right.
• Usually open.

Dumfries and Galloway

✤ MOFFAT CHAPEL OF ST CUTHBERT
[OS NT073055]

Chapel Farm
Moffat DG10 9SB

The farm is located to the west of the town of Moffat. On entering Moffat from the south, take the signs on the left to the golf club; Chapel Farm is about half a mile up the hill on the right. Park carefully away from the farm – and remember that this is a working farm.

Bibliography

MAIN SOURCES

Special mention should go to Aileen Ball who recently translated the 1185 inquest and supplied me with an electronic version that I was able to use as a searchable database of Templar properties.

Addison, Charles G. (1843), *The History of the Knights Templars*, London.

Ball, Aileen (2005), *The 1185 Inquest of the Knights Templar in England* , CD-ROM, South Witham, South Witham Archaeological Group.

Beamon, Sylvia P. (1992), *The Royston Cave: Used by Saints or Sinners? Local Historical Influences of the Templar and Hospitaller Movements*, Baldock, Courtney.

Lord, Evelyn (2002), *The Knights Templar in Britain*, Harlow, Longman.

Nicholson, Helen *(2001), The Knights Templar: A New History*, Stroud, Sutton.

Tull, George F. (2000), *The Traces of the Templars*, The King's England Press.

I also found various editions of the Victoria County History useful: *Berkshire, Buckinghamshire, Cambridgeshire, Essex, Hampshire, Hertfordshire, Kent, Leicestershire, Lincolnshire, Oxfordshire, Somerset, Surrey, Sussex, Warwickshire* and *Yorkshire*. Accessed through British History online. http://www.british-history.ac.uk/

LOCAL BOOKS, GUIDEBOOKS AND LEAFLETS

The most invaluable resource in writing this book has been local research, from the immense work done by Eileen Gooder and Sylvia Beamon to the leaflets available locally.

London

Philip Blewett (1977), *All Hallows by the Tower*, London, Pitkin Pictorials.

Godwin, George (1954), *The Middle Temple: The Society and Fellowship*, London, Staples Press.

Hewitt J. (1863), *An Inscribed Coffin Lid in the Ancient Cemetery of the Temple Church London*, Archaeological Journal.

Robinson, Joseph (1997), *Temple Church*, Andover, Pitkin Guides.

The Southeast

Andrews, D. (ed) (1997), *Cressing Temple: A Guide*, Essex, Essex County Council, [available at site].

Beamon, Sylvia, *Exploring Royston Cave*, [guidebook from cave bookshop, Royston, available at site].

Beldam, Joseph Esq., F.S.A. (1858), *The Origin and Use of the Royston Cave: Being the substance of a report some time since presented to the Royal Society of Antiquaries*, Royston, John Warren.

Excell, Stanley P. (1979), *Sompting Parish Church: A Brief Guide*, Sompting, Friends of Sompting Church, [available at site].

Houldcroft, P.T. (1998), *Pictorial Guide to Royston Cave*, Royston and District Local History Society, [from cave bookshop, Royston, available at site].

Long, E.T. (1941, revised 1978 by Dickenson, M.E.), 'Bisham Abbey: A House of the Knights Templars founded in Stephen's reign'. From the *Countryside Magazine*.

Rigold, S.E. (1962), *Temple Manor, Strood, Rochester, Kent*, London, H.M.S.O., [available at site].

Vardon, T.J., *A Guide to Temple Ewell Church Kent*.

The Southwest

A Brief History of the Panel Painting, [leaflet at site].

Aston, Mick and Taylor, Tim (1996), *Time Team 96: The Site Reports*, London, Channel 4 Television.

Brown, J.R. (1883), *History of the Temple Church, near Bodmin, Cornwall, built by the Knights Templar*, Wadebridge, M. Quintrell.

Cargill, W.D.J. (1953) *The Knights Hospitaller and their Preceptory of Trebeigh in Cornwall*, Oxford, private research paper.

Courtney, R.A. (1914), *Cornwall: The Evolution of the Wheel Cross*, Penzance, Beare and Son.

Langdon, Andrew (2005), *Stone Crosses in East Cornwall: (including parts of Bodmin Moor)*, 2nd ed. rev. and updated, St Austell, Federation of Old Cornwall Societies.

Stark, Rev. Edwin (1984), *Blisland Church: A Guide*.

The Midlands

Fairbairn, F.R. (1938), *The Knights of the Temple and of St. John of Jerusalem and their Connection with Temple Balsall*, [reprinted and available at Temple Balsall church].

Gooder, Eileen (1995),*Temple Balsall: The Warwickshire Preceptory of the Templars and Their Fate*, Chichester, Phillimore.

(1972), *Temple Balsall:A Short History*, published by Friends of Temple Balsall, [available at site].

Pye, Graham (2004), *A Guide to the Church of St. Nicholas Great Wilbraham*, [available at site].

Wood, Richard (2003), *Denny Abbey and the Farmland Museum Cambridgeshire*, London, English Heritage, [available at site].

Lincolnshire

The Knights Templar at Temple Bruer and Aslackby, Lincolnshire Museums Information Sheet. Archaeological Series Number 25.

Atkin, Wendy J. (date unknown), *An Account of the Rise and Fall of the Knights Templar in Lincolnshire*. [Paper submitted to gain a certificate in Local History.]

Dean, John (April, 1997), 'Ritual Protection Marks in Norfolk: A Recent Survey'. [A paper compiled for the Vernacular Architecture Group Spring Conference, Norwich.

Marshall, Graham (ed) (2005), *Historical Aslackby: A Brief Guide for the Visitor*, Aslackby, Pigsty Press.

Mills, D. (date unknown), *The Knights Templar in Kesteven*, [S.l.], North Kesteven District Council.

Owen, Dorothy (1971), *Church and Society in Medieval Lincolnshire*, Lincoln,History of Lincolnshire Committee, Lincolnshire Local History Society.

Platts, Graham (1985), *Land and People in Medieval Lincolnshire*, Lincoln, History of Lincolnshire Committee for the Society for Lincolnshire History and Archaeology.

Yorkshire

Goodricke, Charles (ed) (1885), *History of the Goodricke Family*, London,

Wales and the Borders

Cowley, F.G. (1993), *Llanmadoc and Cheriton: Two North Gower Churches and their Parishes*, Llanmadoc, The Rector and the Llanmadoc and Cheriton Parochial Church Council, [available at site].

Tapper, Audrey (2001), *St. Michaels Church Garway: a Visitor's Guide*, [available at site].

(2001), *Garway 2000: A Brief History of Christianity, 500 – 2000*, [available at site].

Scotland

Rosslyn Chapel (The Official Guidebook), The Earl of Rosslyn, The Rosslyn Chapel Trust. [available at site].

Coutts, RevAlfred (1890), 'The Knights Templars in Scotland', from the Scottish Church Historical Society.

GENERAL BOOKS

Ackroyd, Peter (2001), *London: The Biography*, London, Vintage.

Asbridge, Thomas (2004), *The First Crusade: A New History*, London, Free Press.

Baigent, Michael, Leigh, Richard and Lincoln, Henry (1982), *The Holy Blood and the Holy Grail*, London, Corgi.

Baigent, Michael and Leigh, Richard (1989), *The Temple and the Lodge*, London, Cape.

Ball, Peter (2002), *The Knights Templar at South Witham*, South Witham, South Witham Archaeological Group.

Barber, Malcolm (1978), *The Trial of the Templars*, Cambridge, Cambridge University Press.

Barber, Malcolm (1994), *The New Knighthood: A History of the Order of the Temple*, Cambridge, Cambridge University Press.

Bartlett, Robert (2004), *The Hanged Man: A Story of Miracle, Memory and Colonialism in the Middle Ages*, Princeton, New Jersey, Princeton University Press.

Begg, Ean C.M. (1985), *The Cult of the Black Virgin*, London, Routledge & Kegan Paul.

Branston, Brian (1974), *The Lost Gods of England*, London, Thames and Hudson.

Browne, Edith A. (1911), *Gothic Architecture*, London, A & C. Black.

Burl, Aubrey (1985), *Megalithic Brittany: A Guide to over 350 Ancient Sites and Monuments*, London, Thames and Hudson.

Clairvaux, Bernard, *In Praise of the New Knighthood: A Treatise on the Knights Templar and the Holy Places of Jerusalem*, trans. M. Conrad Greenia, with an introduction by Malcolm Barber (2000), Kalamazoo, Michican and Coalville, Leicestershire, Cistercian Publications.

Danziger, Danny and Gillingham, John (2003), *1215: The Year of Magna Carta*, London, Hodder & Stoughton.

Demurger, Alain (2004), *The Last Templar: The Tragedy of Jacques de Molay, Last Grand Master of the Temple*, trans. by Antonia Nevill, London, Profile Books.

Eco, Umberto (1989), *Foucault's Pendulum*, trans. by William Weaver, London, Secker & Warburg.

Edbury, Pete W. (1994), *The Kingdom of Cyprus and the Crusades, 1191-1374*, Cambridge, Cambridge University Press.

Ereira, Alan and Jones, Terry (1994), *Crusades*, London, BBC Books.

Fisk, Robert (June 20, 2005), 'Why Ridley Scott's Story of the Crusades Struck Such a Chord in a Lebanese Cinema', from *The Independent*, London.

Fitchen, John (1961), *The Construction of Gothic Cathedrals: A Study of Medieval Vault Erection*, Oxford, Clarendon Press.

Gardiner, Philip, with Osborn, Gary (2005), *The Serpent Grail: The Truth Behind the Holy Grail, the Philosopher's Stone and the Elixir of Life*, London, Watkins.

Gilmour-Bryson, Anne (1998), *The Trial of the Templars in Cyprus: A Complete English Edition*, Leiden, Brill.

Greenhill, F.A. (1976) *Incised Effigial Slabs: A study of Engraved Stone Memorials in Latin Christendom, c.1100 to c.1700*, 2 vols, London, Faber.

Guerber, H.A. (1911) *Myths and Legends of the Middle Ages*, [S.I], Harrap.

Haggard, H. Rider (1911), *Red Eve*, Leipzig, B. Tauchnitz.

Hale, Revd. Dr. S.S.G. (Easter 2005), 'Temple Farm – The End of an Era', from the *Beauceant Journal Order of the Temple of Jerusalem*, Ramsgate, Kent.

Hallam, Elizabeth (ed) (1996), *Chronicles of the Crusades: Eye-witness Accounts of the Wars between Christianity and Islam*, Godalming, Bramley.

Hapgood, Charles H. (1966), *Maps of the Ancient Sea Kings: Evidence of Advanced Civilization in the Ice Age*, Philadelphia, Chilton Books.

Hay Richard Augustin (1835), *Genealogie of the Saintclaires of Rosslyn, including the Chartulary of Rosslyn*, Edinburgh, T.G. Stevenson.

James, M.R. (1984 edn.), *The Complete Ghost Stories of M.R. James*, Harmondsworth, Penguin.

Jenkins, Simon (1999), *England's Thousand Best Churches*, London, Allen Lane.

Jerman, James and Wier, Anthony (1986), *Images of Lust: Sexual Carvings on Medieval Churches*, London, Batsford.

Knight, Christopher and Lomas, Robert (1997), *The Second Messiah: Templars, the Turin Shroud and the Great Secret of Freemasonry*, London, Century.

Laidler, Keith (1999), *The Head of God: The Lost Treasure of the Templars*, London, Orion.

Lawrence, T. E. (1910), *Crusader Castles*, London, England: Michael Haag Limited; [New York: dist. by] Hippocrene Books, c1986.

Lees, Beatrice A. (ed) (1935), *Records of the Templars in England in the Twelfth Century: The Inquest of 1185 with Illustrative Charters and Documents*, London, Humphrey Milford, Oxford University Press, for the British Academy.

MacCullough, J.A. (1932), *Medieval Faith and Fable*, London, Harrap.

Martin, Sean (2004), *The Knights Templar*, London, No Exit Press.

Mayes, Philip (ed) (2002), *Excavations at a Templar Preceptory: South Witham, Lincolnshire, 1965–67*, Leeds, The Society for Medieval Archaeology.

Napier, Gordon (2003), *The Rise and Fall of the Knights Templar: The Order of the Temple 1118-1314: A True History of Faith, Glory, Betrayal and Tragedy*, Staplehurst, Spellmount.

Nicholson, Helen (1993), *Templars, Hospitallers, and Teutonic Knights: Images of the Military Orders, 1128-1291*, Leicester, Leicester University Press.

Oliver, Rev. (1841–42), 'Temple Bruer', from *A Selection of Papers Relative to the County of Lincoln*, Lincoln, Lincolnshire Topographical Society,

Partner, Peter (1990), *The Knights Templar & Their Myth*, rev. edn. Rochester, Vermont, Destiny Books.

Picknett, Lynn and Prince, Clive (1997), *The Templar Revelation: Secret Guardians of the True Identity of Christ*, London, Bantam.

Picknett, Lynn and Prince, Clive (2000, new edn.), *Turin Shroud: In Whose Image? How Leonardo da Vinci Fooled History*, London, Corgi.

IN SEARCH OF THE KNIGHTS TEMPLAR

Plomer, William (ed) (1938), *Kilvert's Diary*, London, Cape.

Pritchard, V. (1967), *English Medieval Graffiti*, Cambridge, Cambridge University Press.

Read, Piers Paul (2001), *The Templars*, London, Phoenix.

Reston, James Jnr (2001), *Warriors of God: Richard the Lionheart and Saladin in the Third Crusade*, London, Faber & Faber.

Riley-Smith, Jonathan (1985), *The First Crusade and the Idea of Crusading*, London, Athlone.

Robinson, David (ed) (1998), *The Cistercian Abbeys of Britain: Far from the Concourse of Men*, London, Batsford.

Robinson, John J. (1991), *Dungeon, Fire and Sword: The Knights Templar in the Crusades*, New York, M. Evans & Co.

St John Hope, W.H. (1843), 'The Round Church of the Knights Templars at Temple Bruer, Lincolnshire', from *A Selection of Papers Relative to the County of Lincoln*, Lincoln, Lincolnshire Topographical Society, 74, 75.

de Sandoli, Sabino (1974), *Corpus Inscriptionum Crucesignatorum Terrae Sanctae (1099-1291): Testo Traduzione e Annotazioni*, Jerusalem, Francisca Printing Press.

Selwood, Dominic (1999), *Knights of the Cloister: Templars and Hospitallers in Central-Southern Occitania, c.1100-c.1300*, Woodbridge, Boydell Press.

Severin, Tim (1990), *Crusader*, with photographs by Peter Essick, London, Arrow.

Seward, Desmond (1972), *The Monks of War: The Military Religious Orders*, London, Eyre Methuen Ltd.

Sinclair, Andrew (2002), *The Sword and the Grail: Of the Grail and the Templars and a True Discovery of America*, Edinburgh, Birlinn.

Sora, Steven (1999), *The Lost Treasure of the Knights Templar: Solving the Oak Island Mystery*, Rochester, Vermont, Destiny Books.

Taylor, Richard (2004), *How to Read a Church: A Guide to Images, Symbols and Meanings in Churches and Cathedrals*, London, Rider.

Vaughan, Richard (ed) (1987), *Chronicles of Matthew Paris: Monastic Life in the Thirteenth Century*, Sutton.

Wilson, Colin *(1984)*, *A Criminal History of Mankind*, London, Granada.

Wood, Herbert (1907), *The Templars in Ireland*, Dublin.

Wood, Michael (2003), *In Search of Shakespeare*, London, BBC Worldwide.

WEBSITES

Church Crawler [details of English churches]
http://www.churchcrawler.co.uk/

The Knights Templar in Britain.
http://www.thecyberfarm.com/templars/templar britain/templarbritainhome.htm

English Heritage
http://www.english-heritage.org.uk/

Templar history
http://www.templarhistory.com/

The Labyrinth: Resources for Medieval Studies: Sponsored by Georgetown University
http://www.georgetown.edu/labyrinth/labyrinth-home.html

Instituto Português do Património Arquitectónico (Portuguese Institute of Architectural Heritage)
http://www.ippar.pt/english/

Ordnance Survey maps
http://www.ordnancesurvey.co.uk/

Knights of the Temple (Part 1&2) By Brian Hoggard
http://www.whitedragon.org.uk

Church orientation – article by Bob Trubshaw [at the edge web magazine]
http://www.indigogroup.co.uk/edge/chorien.htm

Chinon Parchment [Barbara Frale]
http://en.wikipedia.org/wiki/Chinon_Parchment

Westford Knight, Templars in America
http://www.tc-lethbridge.com

The Catholic Encyclopaedia at:
http://www.newadvent.org/

MEDIA

'The Knights Templar' [2000] Beckman videos.

'The Knights Templar at South Witham'. by South Witham Archaeological Group (SWAG)

Index

IN SEARCH OF THE KNIGHTS TEMPLAR

Acknowledgements

I would like to thank:

Terry Welbourn; Colin and Joy Wilson; Peter and Aileen Ball; Tim Staniland; Christophe Staf; Janet Holmshaw at Middlesex University; Cressida Finch and Pamela Willis at St. John's library, Clerkenwell; Sylvia Beamon; Anne and Michael Bucknell; Chris and Bron Brighton; Paul Lang, St Bernard's Hospital, Librarian Hanwell

I would like to thank the following for their assistance at individual sites

Emma Clarke-Bolton for English Heritage; Rui Ferreira at Convento de Cristo; Robin Griffith-Jones, Master of the Temple, and Brian Nicholson, verger, Temple Church, London; David Driscoll and Lynne Smith at All Hallows by the Tower; Alison Heald and Brett Dolman at Curator's Department, the Tower of London; Medway Council and staff at Strood Manor; Peter Mann at Bisham Abbey; Celia Walpole, Town Clerk, Royston Cave museum curator Peter Houldcroft; Kerry Cullen and staff at Four Pillars Hotel, Sandford; South Witham Archaeological Group; Chris Gudgin and Graham Marshall, Aslackby; Lynn Snelson, Dean's Secretary at Lincoln Cathedral; Mal Stainforth and Lesley Dean at Lincoln Castle; Charles & Mrs Dent, Ribston Hall; Mrs E. Eltringham at Temple Hirst; Helen Duce at Ludlow Castle; Janet and Andrew Clift for Garway; Viv Grimshawe at Llanmadoc, and Bernice Cardy, Swansea Museum; Mrs Rosalind Caird, Hereford Cathedral Library; Sarah C. Jones, Historic Scotland Assistant Events and Filming Manager; Stuart Beattie, Project Director, Rosslyn Chapel; Mr and Mrs Hutchinson, Chapel Farm, Moffat; Ian Howie-Willis, Priory Librarian, St John Ambulance – Australia.

I would particularly like to thank:

Matt Lowing and Michael Dover at Weidenfeld. Christine King, editor, for going beyond the call of duty. Sheila Ableman, agent, for her confidence in this project and its author, from day one. And of course my wife Sandy, without whose support this book would have never have existed.

PICTURE CREDITS: **All pictures © Simon Brighton with the exception of:** p. 14, 24 and 29 © The Bridgeman Art Library; p 15 (left) © Joanna Cannon (www.JoannaCannon.com); p. 25 © Hulton Archive / Getty Images; p. 27 and 28 © Interfoto.de; p. 89 and p 150 (top and bottom) English Heritage; p. 114 © akg images / Erich Lessing **All site photos by Simon Brighton, access to sites and permission for photography as follows:** p. 33 and 39 permission from the director of the Convento de Cristo; p. 42 by permission of St John's Museum Clerkenwell; p. 52 The Revd Bertrand Olivier, The Revd Canon David Driscoll, All Hallows by the Tower, Byward Street, London; p. 55 Trustees of the British Museum; p. 56 London Temple (permission given by the Honourable Societies of the Inner and Middle Temples); p. 64 Tower of London, Historic Royal Palaces; p. 68 Royston Cave, Royston Town Council Town Hall, Royston. Cave curator Peter Houldcroft; p. 76 English Heritage; p. 78 Medway Council / English Heritage; p. 81 English Heritage; p. 86 Cressing Temple / Essex County Council; p. 90 Bisham Abbey / English National Sports Centres; p. 106 ground plan of Temple Church, Bristol, permission of English Heritage; p. 120 from 'History of the Temple Church'; p. 128 Denny Abbey (English Heritage); p. 136 Rothley Court Hotel; p. 138 Oxford Thames Four Pillars Hotel; p. 151 top and bottom, English Heritage; p. 170 The Angel & Royal Hotel, High Street, Grantham, Lincolnshire; p. 174 Dean and chapter of Lincoln Cathedral; p. 178 Friends of Lincoln Castle & Lincolnshire County Council Heritage Services; p. 182 English Heritage; p. 188 The Dent family, Ribston Hall; p. 192 Temple Manor Nursing Home; p. 196 English Heritage; p. 208 Dean and chapter of Hereford Cathedral; p. 210 Ludlow Castle, Earl of Powis and the Trustees of the Powis Castle Estate; p. 216 Scotland: Temple, Kilmartin and Kilmory by permission of Historic Scotland; p. 224 bottom right, permission from Director, Convento de Cristo; p. 232 Rosslyn Chapel Trust, Rosslyn Chapel, Roslin, Midlothian.

The publishers would be pleased to rectify any errors brought to their notice at the earliest possible opportunity.

A PHOENIX PAPERBACK

First published in Great Britain in 2006 by Weidenfeld & Nicolson This paperback edition published in 2008 by Phoenix Illustrated, an imprint of Orion Books Ltd, Orion House, 5 Upper St Martin's Lane, London WC2H 9EA

An Hachette Livre UK company

10 9 8 7 6 5 4 3 2 1

Copyright © Simon Brighton 2006 Pictures copyright © Simon Brighton, except as indicated above. Design and layout © Weidenfeld & Nicolson 2006

The right of the copyholders to be identified as the authors of this work has been asserted by them in accordance with the Copyright, Designs and Patents Act 1988.

A CIP catalogue record for this book is available from the British Library.

ISBN 978-0-7538-2228-9

Printed and bound by Cayfosa (Impresia Iberica)

The Orion Publishing Group's policy is to use papers that are natural, renewable and recyclable products and made from wood grown in sustainable forests. The logging and manufacturing processes are expected to conform to the environmental regulations of the country of origin.

www.orionbooks.co.uk